The Synchronous Trainer's Survival Guide

Facilitating Successful Live and Online Courses, Meetings, and Events

Jennifer Hofmann

Pfeiffer

A Wiley Imprint
www.pfeiffer.com

Published by Pfeiffer
An Imprint of Wiley
989 Market Street, San Francisco, CA 94103-1741   www.pfeiffer.com

For additional copies/bulk purchases of this book in the U.S. please contact 800-274-4434.

Pfeiffer books and products are available through most bookstores. To contact Pfeiffer directly
call our Customer Care Department within the U.S. at 800-274-4434, outside the U.S. at
317-572-3985 or fax 317-572-4002 or www.pfeiffer.com.

Pfeiffer also publishes its books in a variety of electronic formats. Some content that appears in
print may not be available in electronic books.

Library of Congress Cataloging-in-Publication Data

Hofmann, Jennifer
The synchronous trainer's survival guide: facilitating successful live and online courses, meetings,
and events / Jennifer Hofmann.
p. cm.
"A Wiley Imprint."
Includes bibliographical references and index.
ISBN 0-7879-6943-5 (alk. paper)
1. Training—Handbooks, manuals, etc. 2. Computer-assisted instruction—Handbooks, manuals,
etc. 3. Internet in education—Handbooks, manuals, etc. I. Title.
LB1027.47.H64 2003
370.113—dc21

2003006668

Acquiring Editor: Lisa Shannon
Director of Development: Kathleen Dolan Davies
Developmental Editor: Susan Rachmeler
Editor: Rebecca Taff
Senior Production Editor: Dawn Kilgore
Manufacturing Supervisor: Bill Matherly
Illustrations: Richard Sheppard

Printed in the United States of America
Printing   10 9 8 7 6 5 4 3 2 1

Contents

Preface   ix

Introduction   1

1 An Introduction to the Synchronous Classroom   7

New Versus Older Delivery Methods • The Synchronous
Classroom • Synchronous Software

2 Facilitating in the Synchronous Classroom   29

Profile of an Effective Synchronous Trainer • The Synchronous
Trainer's Workstation • The Producer • Leader Guides for
Trainer/Producer Collaboration

3 Communicating in the Synchronous Classroom   49

Using Visuals • Using Your Voice • Language Tips • Gauging
Participation • Using the Collaboration Tools
• A Note on Class Size • Rules of Thumb

4 Synchronous Classroom Management   70

Managing Time and Scheduling Issues • Determining
the Best Length for a Program • Communicating with
Class Participants • Preparing to Facilitate the Class • Using
Your Leader Guide Effectively

5 Managing the Technology   83

Creating a Seamless Production • Troubleshooting Technology

6 Working with Synchronous Participants   98

The Participant Experience • Learning How to Learn Online •
Ground Rules • The Effective Learning Environment •
Participant Guides

7 Synchronous Events   109

eMeetings • Expert Q&A • Webinars • Learning
Events • A Final Thought

Appendices   115

A. Synchronous Software Features Checklist   117

B. Synchronous Classroom Management Checklists   121

C. Recommended Resources for Synchronous and
   Blended e-Learning   125

D. A Glossary of Terms   127

About the Author   133

Index   135

Pfeiffer Publications Guide   141

List of Figures and Tables

Figure 1.1   Traditional, Asynchronous, and Synchronous
Delivery Methods   8

Table 1.1   Common Synchronous Features and Their
Uses   15

Figure 2.1   Sample Page Mockup   46

Figure 4.1   Timing Milestone in a Synchronous Leader
Guide   79

Figure 4.2   Highlighted Script   80

Figure 4.3   Notes Separated from Action Steps   81

Figure 5.1   Windows Display Properties: Screen Resolution
Settings   85

Figure 5.2   Virtual Classroom Window and Chat Area   86

Table 5.1   Keystrokes   87

Figure 6.1   Sample Participant Guide Table of Contents 104

Figure 7.1   Synchronous Event Continuum   110

I tell you and you forget.
I show you and you remember.
I involve you and you understand.
—Eric Butterworth

Preface

I have been working with Internet-based synchronous (live and on-line) learning technologies since 1996—truly an old hand for a field so new! During this time I've had the opportunity to utilize many different software platforms and watch this niche of the training market grow. The technology has been catching up to the potential of the delivery medium, and these "virtual classrooms" are becoming not only accepted but expected as part of an organization's training offerings.

As a traditional instructional designer and trainer I was frustrated by the lack of direction given to new online trainers. The fact that different skills and techniques were needed to succeed in this environment was often overlooked, and trainers had no learning opportunities besides "point-and-click" software training. Everyone was learning by experience—often hard-fought—and there did not seem to be any single place for capturing best practices and lessons learned. Another issue seemed to be that organizations were treating synchronous implementations as technology initiatives and not as change initiatives.

I often refer to *The Synchronous Trainer's Survival Guide* as my "diary of things that went wrong and how I fixed them for the next time." I captured my team's real-life lessons learned and documented the techniques. As the training community learns and develops best practices, this guide will be updated. If you would like to contribute to future publications, please complete the feedback form at the end of the guide.

Acknowledgments

No project is the result of a single person's effort. This guide represents collaboration and teamwork over several years.

Thank you to the following synchronous training vendors for allowing us to use screen shots from their products to illustrate points throughout this guide:

- Centra and the CentraOne™ product (www.centra.com)
- EDT Learning and the LearnLinc™ product (www.learnlinc.com)
- Elluminate and the vClass™ product (www.elluminate.com)
- HorizonLive and the HorizonLive™ product (www.horizonlive.com)
- Interwise and the InterWise Millenium™ product (www.interwise.com)
- PlaceWare and the PlaceWare™ product (www.placeware.com)

My colleagues have provided support and offered many ideas. Thanks especially to Amy Avergun, Phylise Banner, Nanette Miner, Elizabeth Tracy, and Ellen Turner-Christian.

My family keeps trying but still doesn't understand quite what I do every day. Perhaps this guide will help them to figure it out.

Finally, I would especially like to thank my clients who, over the years, have allowed my team to experiment and have trusted that we would find the best training solutions.

May 2003   JENNIFER HOFMANN

Introduction

The primary audience for this guide is trainers and other group facilitators who are beginning to deliver content using a synchronous classroom. One goal is to provide information that you can use immediately to make your synchronous events successful.

When discussing Internet learning technologies, "synchronous" refers to training that is delivered to a geographically dispersed group of participants at the same time. Once the evolution of synchronous training technologies kicked into high gear during the late 1990s, the face of training and education changed forever. We now have the ability to deliver live, interactive training to anyone with access to a computer and a phone line. Collaborative tools allow for engaging interaction among experts, trainers, and participants. The interface of the "virtual classroom" becomes much more than a substitute for a live trainer—it represents the nature of the content and the participants in ways that can be creative and educationally sound. It reduces the need for travel to training events, and it can save an organization a substantial amount in expenses.

The technologies have a much wider reach than the classroom. Conference calls are quickly being replaced by "eMeetings." The same principles that can make synchronous learning events effective apply to these meetings as well. Dispersed teams can communicate and collaborate with a visual interface at a relatively low cost. This type of interaction can make online meetings much more productive than traditional conference calls. Every member of the team can bring his or her own content and share it with everyone by using application and content sharing tools.

What if you want to reach thirty, fifty, or one hundred participants—or more? "eConferences" hold an answer for you. Experts provide lectures, and participants use a variety of communication tools to ask questions and provide feedback.

These corporate and educational uses are just the beginning. I once attended a baby shower in a virtual classroom for a woman who lived in Connecticut but worked on a virtual team. Attendees were in Massachusetts, New Hampshire, and Georgia! (Yes, there was cake!)

History of Learning Technologies

While the focus of this guide is on trainers as they deal with the emerging field of synchronous online training and learning, it is important to remember that this technology is only one in a long history of learning technologies.

Since the introduction of correspondence schools, every communication innovation has held the promise of being the ultimate solution to educating everyone who needed it—whenever and wherever they needed it. Even as early as when motion pictures first hit the screen, innovative thinkers anxiously anticipated the day we would no longer need to go to a classroom and education would be recorded and available for all posterity.

The thinking was the same throughout the 20th Century. Veterans of training and education remember, often not fondly, the introductions of audiotapes, videotapes, teleconferencing, interactive television, CD-ROM, and finally, the World Wide Web to the education arena. Each innovation brought the need for a technology investment on the part of organizations, trainers, instructional designers, and the ultimate audience—the participants.

Often, these technologies did not seem to reach their potential. The reasons were numerous. Sometimes the intended audience did not have access to the necessary technology. Sometimes the content did not seem to fit the technology. More often than not, the people involved (instructional designers, trainers, and participants) did not have the new skills and understanding they needed to support and participate in the training process.

The 21st Century offers still more exciting innovations for training and education professionals. Newer and friendlier software and greater bandwidth have made more training technologies available to more audiences. Now we can combine the technologies of correspondence, audio, video, and graphical interfaces with live trainers and group collaboration. This live aspect of technology-based training is commonly referred to as "synchronous" learning.

With these options comes a trend toward "blended" learning technologies. This term refers to a combination—or blend—of different learning methods. In other words, blended learning allows you to use the best combination of learning technologies to meet all of your training objectives.

On the surface, we seem to have finally discovered the cure— *the* approach to learning technologies. By adding synchronous options to our technology toolbox, we allow social contact with the trainer and other participants. But veterans cannot help but wonder: Have we discovered the cure-all, or are we opening yet another Pandora's box? Will we be expected to master all of these new technologies? Where is the proof that they are effective? Will we be given the time and resources to develop the necessary skills to create high-quality learning experiences? What skills will make trainers successful? This guide is intended to provide answers to some of these questions for you, the trainer.

Moving to Virtual Classrooms

The most common error for newcomers to the synchronous training arena is assuming that the same rules that apply in a traditional classroom apply in a synchronous classroom. This is understandable, especially since many similar components exist. In practice, however, the resemblance is only skin-deep.

An analogy can be drawn between synchronous training and the introduction of television in the 1950s. The creators of television naturally assumed that television should mimic a theater production. Not surprisingly, early TV did just that. There was a single set that changed between scenes, one camera that maintained the same angle throughout, and a live audience. Of course, it did not take people long to realize that what played well in Peoria did not necessarily play well on television. A new metaphor needed to be developed for the new medium—one that incorporated the aspects of theater but also took advantage of the special features that were available.

This guide can help you, the trainer, transition away from the traditional practices of delivering classroom training. Just as putting the stage on television did not take advantage of that technology, trying to force a traditional classroom design and delivery method into the synchronous classroom is very limiting.

The similarities between synchronous training and a broadcast production do not end with this story. In fact, I use the broadcast production metaphor throughout this guide. Synchronous programs often use live event technical support to keep everything running smoothly. A producer (often called an "assistant trainer") can be instrumental in supporting instruction.

How This Guide Is Organized

Many factors contribute to effective training events: personal readiness of both learner and trainer, the ability to control the technology and the people interacting in the technology, and the use of activities that support the content and are effective in the environment. With this in mind, this guide is organized into the following chapters:

Chapter 1—An Introduction to the Synchronous Classroom. After explaining how synchronous training can fit into your overall mix, this chapter provides a detailed overview of the collaboration and facilitation features available in most synchronous training platforms and includes suggestions for instructional applications of each.

Chapter 2—Facilitating in the Synchronous Classroom. This chapter covers effective synchronous trainer traits, provides tips and techniques for facilitating programs, and explains the ins and outs of working with a "producer."

Chapter 3—Communicating in the Synchronous Classroom. This chapter describes how common elements of communication— voice, visuals, language, and participant cues—are different in the synchronous environment. Various collaboration tools are also explained.

Chapter 4—Synchronous Classroom Management. This chapter provides techniques for managing time, presents some additional communication techniques, explains how to prepare for a synchronous event, and gives hints for effective use of a leader guide.

Chapter 5—Managing the Technology. This chapter provides guidelines for minimizing technical issues and for troubleshooting those issues when they do come up.

Chapter 6—Working with Synchronous Participants. This chapter provides tips on maximizing the participant experience.

Chapter 7—Synchronous Events. This chapter gives some direction for what should be considered when designing synchronous programs, especially different events such as eMeetings, expert presentations, and learning events.

Appendix. The appendix provides several checklists, a glossary, and a list of resources that may help you with your synchronous initiative.

At the end of each chapter is a page for you to capture any questions, ideas, or applications related to what you just read. I encourage you to keep track of these items.

You may choose to jump around the book to get right to the information you need. If you are new to the synchronous environment, however, you should read Chapter 1, An Introduction to the Synchronous Classroom, first so that you understand the basics before jumping right in.

There is a feedback form at the end of the book. I encourage you to use that form to compile all of your questions and send them to me. I will be happy to help you—and potentially incorporate the answers and your ideas into the next edition of this book.

If you have never attended a synchronous session before, I strongly suggest you attend one or two prior to reading the book, and especially before putting what you read in this book into action. It will help you to visualize the environment and give you some context for the recommendations I make. If courses are offered within your organization, start there. If not, go to the website of your synchronous vendor and enroll in any public courses they may be offering.

A Note About Terminology

For the purpose of consistency, I have chosen specific words throughout this guide. For instance, I use the term "trainer" throughout, whereas you might use "instructor" or "teacher." I use the word "participant," but you might use "learner" or "student."

You will also notice that I use the term "learning technologies" instead of "training technologies" and "learning event" instead of "training event." This helps me to reinforce the reason I am in this industry: to create environments in which participants can learn. I believe that the learning outcome should be foremost in our minds; the delivery method is simply a means to an end.

Please refer to the glossary at the end of this guide to clarify any terms with which you may not be familiar.

1

An Introduction to the Synchronous Classroom

I once heard the synchronous classroom described as "the best and worst combination of traditional classroom training and asynchronous (self-paced) web-based training (WBT)." There is quite a bit of truth to this statement. As training professionals, our task is to "accentuate the positive and eliminate the negative." That is, we need to take advantage of the features of the synchronous classroom that make it unlike any training technology that has come before. Before you do that, you'll need to master the basics of working with this technology. Figure 1.1 shows how synchronous training compares with asynchronous and traditional programs.

New Versus Older Delivery Methods

Let's start by comparing and contrasting the synchronous classroom with traditional and asynchronous classrooms.

Traditional Instruction

Traditional classrooms are characterized by the trainer and participants being in the same place at the same time and involved in the same activities. The trainer uses common tools such as overhead projectors, whiteboards, and flip charts to assist in delivering content.

FIGURE 1.1   Traditional, Asynchronous, and Synchronous Delivery Methods.

Traditional

Asynchronous

Synchronous

The advantages of the traditional classroom are many. The most important advantage is that most people are comfortable learning in this environment. We don't need to explain to participants how they should interact, behave, and learn. Participants can ask questions immediately. A sense of community can be developed. Participants often appreciate being able to leave their regular workplace and learn in a new setting.

The trainer also knows how to manage this environment. Eye contact and body language are important indicators to the trainer and help to direct pace and communication.

This method of instruction does have its drawbacks. Classroom space is often available only at a premium. Shorter programs often are not delivered because they are not deemed worthwhile due to the distance participants must travel, the cost of renting a classroom, or the cost of paying a trainer. Because of the logistics and costs involved, many programs never have a chance to be delivered.

Asynchronous Instruction

"Asynchronous" refers to instruction that is not constrained by geography or time. Everyone involved in an asynchronous activity performs his or her part on his or her own time. Often, this is also called "self-paced" training. Examples include books, CD-ROM tutorials, web-based tutorials, videotapes, audiotapes, and discussion boards. Asynchronous instruction may be trainer-led (as in the case of moderated discussion boards) or self-directed (as in the case of CD-ROM tutorials).

The primary advantage of asynchronous programs is their convenience. Participants can complete assignments when they want and where they want (as long as they have access to the appropriate technologies). Information can be processed at a pace appropriate to the individual participant.

Asynchronous learning has many disadvantages as well. Participants can find it difficult to motivate themselves to complete these programs. Without specific deadlines and deliverables, it is hard to keep self-directed training high on a priority list. If a participant has trouble understanding something, it can be very frustrating not to be able to ask questions of a "live" trainer.

Synchronous Instruction

"Synchronous" refers to instruction that is led by a facilitator in real time, generally over the Internet. (Many would argue that traditional classrooms are synchronous as well.) Examples of synchronous interactions include conference calls, instant messaging, videoconferences, whiteboard sessions, and synchronous classrooms. Synchronous learning is characterized by group interaction and collaboration among participants. Discussion and problem solving can be managed using a variety of methods, and people in different cultures and personal situations can be involved at the same time from wherever they choose.

Problems encountered with synchronous instruction often start with the technology. If installation problems occur, participants begin the experience with a negative impression. Some people (participants and trainers) have difficulty believing the synchronous classroom can be as effective as a traditional classroom, and so do not fully commit to active participation. Because of the relative infancy of the technology, trainers and participants are all trying to cope in spite of insufficient experience.

Blended Instruction

This term refers to a combination—or blend—of different learning technologies and methods. Blended learning is becoming increasingly common with the availability of both synchronous and asynchronous learning options. An example may be a course that consists of an asynchronous web module that covers content and a follow-up synchronous module that allows participants to apply the content and ask questions.

It is becoming apparent to many practitioners that the blended formats are best to accommodate different learning styles and to best support learning objectives. Because of this, trainers will often need to manage a combination of traditional, asynchronous, and synchronous training technologies.

The Synchronous Classroom

When Should You Use a Synchronous Classroom?

Use a virtual classroom when:

- *Real-time interaction with experts is critical.* When participants need to have questions answered before they can move on or the trainer must observe that a skill has been mastered, use a live environment.

- *Face-to-face interaction is NOT critical.* Some programs require that the trainer be in the same room with participants in order for the program to be successful. "Lab" courses for hardware specialists (physically building computer systems) might be a good example. However, pre-lab and post-lab lectures might be conducted in an online format. This would be a great opportunity to blend training technologies.

- *Your audience is dispersed throughout a large geographic area.* If participants are not all located in the same place, synchronous events minimize travel time and expenses.

- *The topic is critical enough that you must ensure that participants complete the training.* If asynchronous instruction may be appropriate for teaching the content, but participants might not feel motivated to complete the asynchronous work, using a synchronous event as a follow-up to asynchronous work might provide the impetus for participants to complete the requirements.

- *You have a new product or an update to an existing product and need to update your workforce.* Use the synchronous environment to get product information out to your sales teams and customers. A combination training/marketing event can inexpensively create value for your clients.

- *Your work group needs to collaborate and can use the collaboration tools.* If you have a geographically dispersed work group that needs to get together to come to consensus, use the synchronous classroom to give the group a chance to share ideas and collaborate.

What Can Be Taught?

Trainers and experts are often concerned that their content is not well-suited for the synchronous environment. To answer the question, "What can be taught?" I examine the instructional objectives of a course. Consider, for example, converting a two-day course with the goal of teaching stand-up presentation skills. Initially, you might think that none of the content is appropriate for synchronous instruction. Before you make a final decision, however, review the individual objectives that support this goal, for example:

At the end of this program, participants will be able to:

1. Identify the traits of an effective presenter;
2. Plan a thirty-minute presentation;
3. Prepare for the thirty-minute presentation; and
4. Effectively deliver a presentation to a group.

Decide whether you can test for completion of these objectives in the synchronous environment. Objectives 1, 2, and 3 do not require the physical presence of an instructor. These objectives can be met using brainstorming, lecture, prerecorded video, and other methods that can be utilized online. Objective 4 is the only one that poses a difficulty. The participants need to be observed in order to be evaluated on this objective. To design this program, you can plan to teach the first three objectives online and then find an alternative for the final objective. Perhaps the trainer can evaluate a videotaped presentation, or perhaps the class can get together for just one day to present and be critiqued. This would save on facility expenses and potentially reduce the time and expense associated with participant travel.

There are many reasons to use a synchronous environment, and many topics that would be appropriate. With experience, you'll find you can design events that you originally thought would not be effective online.

Synchronous Software

If you have ever attended a synchronous classroom software demonstration, you have seen software vendors dazzle prospects by demonstrating endless application features. Many of these features are similar across platforms, but there are some important variations to bear in mind. Often the same features differ markedly from product to product. Consider the whiteboard feature as an example. In some synchronous products, all participants and the trainer can use a whiteboard at the same time. In some, only one person can access it at a time. In still others, only a trainer can access it. But despite the differences, all of these vendors can accurately state that they have whiteboard capabilities.

It's up to you to experiment and get to the heart of each feature. As you prepare for your synchronous program, make it a priority to master the potential of these powerful options.

Vendors

Over the past five years, I have used many synchronous software platforms, including Centra's Symposium (www.centra.com), EDT's LearnLinc (www.mentergy.com), Elluminate's vClass (www. elluminate.com), Interwise (www.interwise.com), HorizonLive (www. horizonlive.com), PlaceWare (www.placeware.com), WebEx (www.webex.com), and others. In order to benefit the largest possible audience, I have written this guide in as generic a way as possible. However, some of the techniques will not work with some synchronous platforms, so I have dedicated some space to alerting you to the differences and providing tips to manage them.

Features and Functionality Defined

Table 1.1 defines the major features of synchronous training packages. It also suggests some instructional uses for each feature that you might not have thought about. The names I have given each feature are intended to be generic—the features might have different names in your software platform. Whenever possible, I have included a graphic to illustrate what the feature may look like. Your platform may also have features not listed here. Taking the time to learn all of the nuances will certainly help you to make your programs more engaging. Practice and explore until you are comfortable with the details.

When appropriate, I have added "considerations" to the instructional uses of some features. When designing activities that utilize these features, you'll need to understand how the features work in your particular synchronous platform. Keep these considerations in mind when designing your own activities. If you are planning to attend training on the software platform, find the time to discuss these considerations with a software expert.

If you have ideas I have not listed, there is a page at the end of this chapter for you to capture them.

For further reference on synchronous training terms, consult the glossary in the Appendix of this guide.

As discussed earlier, your particular platform may have additional features. For example, you may be able to automatically bring up photographs of whoever is speaking. The trainer may be able to sneak a peak at an individual participant's desktop. Different participant interfaces may be available for individuals who speak different languages. Every new release of every platform introduces us to something new, so make sure you keep up-to-date and continue to practice.

The Appendix contains a features checklist that you can use to capture specific information about your synchronous platform. Use this checklist to help you to document the ins and outs of your particular training platform. Bring it to synchronous software training and ask your trainer questions, or spend the time to investigate on our own.

TABLE 1.1. Common Synchronous Features and Their Uses

SYNCHRONOUS FEATURE: AUDIO

One-way or two-way audio is available in most synchronous packages. Audio can be delivered via the Internet (VOIP) or by a phone bridge (audioconferencing). When VOIP is used, sending audio is often initiated by pressing the <Crtl> key on your keyboard.

Some organizations opt not to utilize the VOIP. For various reasons, they find audio-conferencing to be a better choice for their organizations.

USES

- The trainer's voice is perhaps the most important content delivery method available in a synchronous classroom. (This will be discussed more in the next chapter.)
- Use the audio as you would in a traditional classroom—lectures, group discussions, and Q&A sessions are all effective in a synchronous classroom once the facilitation techniques have been mastered.

Centra Audio Controls

CONSIDERATIONS

- What type of audio (full-duplex, half-duplex, telephone conferencing) is available?
- Does the software have some kind of "wizard" to test audio settings?

SYNCHRONOUS FEATURE: CHAT

Text-based chat allows the participants and trainer to communicate with one another through text messaging. Private messaging allows participants to signal difficulties without disrupting a session.

Often, chat discussions (or transcripts) can be saved as text files and used after the event is over.

USES

- Participants who are more reserved are often more likely to interact when text chat options are available.
- Questions can be "parked" to be answered later—either during or after the class session.
- You can conduct brainstorming sessions in the chat room.
- If you have a technical support person online, he or she can monitor the chat to identify and fix technical problems without interrupting the class. If you happen to be using a subject-matter expert, he or she can monitor a classroom in order to answer content-related questions that may be out of the scope of the current lecture or activity.

TABLE 1.1. Common Synchronous Features and Their Uses, Cont'd.

- Independent or group exercise instructions can be pasted from a word processor into a chat area for participants to review during an exercise.
- Some software platforms offer group chat areas, while others have features that more closely resemble an Instant Messenger function (sometimes called "Notes").

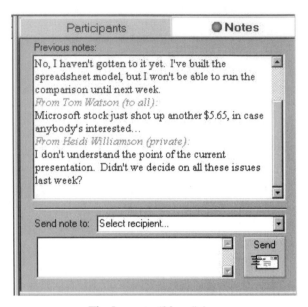

The Interwise "Notes" Area

CONSIDERATIONS

- Is full group chat available?
- Is private messaging to the trainer/assistant trainer available?
- Is private messaging between participants allowed?
- Can a transcript of chat conversations be saved?
- Does the transcript include private messaging?

SYNCHRONOUS FEATURE: BREAKOUT ROOMS

This feature allows small groups to meet and share information during a larger synchronous session.

USES

- Breakout rooms are ideal for training sessions in which teams or groups can share specific content.
- Participants can be assigned to individual breakout rooms to complete a self-paced exercise or assessment.

TABLE 1.1. Common Synchronous Features and Their Uses, Cont'd.

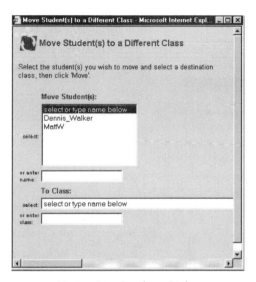

HorizonLive Breakout Dialog

- Team competitions can be conducted.
- You can work with groups or individuals on an as-needed basis.
- Different groups can work with different content or on different exercises.
- If there are varying levels of expertise in a class, a program can be divided and different trainers can moderate the breakout rooms.
- Breakout room instructions need to be very clear, since the trainer is not always available.

CONSIDERATIONS
- What features (whiteboards, application sharing, and so forth) are available in the breakout rooms?
- Can participants be pre-assigned to a particular room?
- Can participants be moved from room to room during an activity?
- Can materials (whiteboards and other items) created in breakout rooms be shared when the large group is reconvened?

SYNCHRONOUS FEATURE: WHITEBOARDS

- Roughly the synchronous equivalent of a traditional flip chart, whiteboards allow trainers and participants to post ideas. The primary difference is that many whiteboards allow multiple people to write at the same time.
- Images can be placed on prepared whiteboards (often in the form of PowerPoint™ slides) ahead of time or pasted during the session.

TABLE 1.1.   Common Synchronous Features and Their Uses, Cont'd.

Some synchronous applications allow users to take a "snapshot" of a part of an application and paste that snapshot to the whiteboard for annotation.

Some whiteboards are "object-oriented," which means each individual drawing can be moved or deleted.

USES

• Use the whiteboard for anything you would use a flip chart or marker board for in a traditional classroom setting. For example, you can capture expectations at the beginning of a class and revisit them at the end of a program.

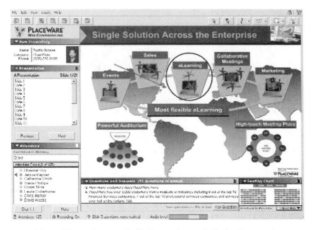

PlaceWare, Inc.—Full Console and Slide Controls

• Content changes and additions can be captured and used to revise the program.

• You can capture participants' ideas in flip-chart style.

• Whiteboards can often be archived for reuse in asynchronous applications or emailed to class participants.

• Content can be highlighted as it is discussed, which makes lectures more meaningful.

• Icebreakers and games can also be created using the whiteboard.

CONSIDERATIONS

• Can you save whiteboards created during the event?

• Can graphics be pasted or imported to the whiteboard?

• How many people can write on the whiteboard at once?

• If you return to a slide that you have written on, will the comments still be there?

TABLE 1.1. Common Synchronous Features and Their Uses, Cont'd.

- What tools are available for whiteboard drawing?
- Can drawing and graphics be moved once they are on the whiteboard?

SYNCHRONOUS FEATURE: SURVEYS/POLLS/FEEDBACK/ HANDRAISING/ PACING/COMPREHENSION

Various devices have been built into synchronous platforms to compensate for the loss of eye contact and body language.

A variety of survey, polling, and feedback tools are available in all platforms. They help you to get a quick check on the pulse of the class and allow the participants to appraise the trainer on the pace and clarity of the content.

USES

- Use surveys and polls to determine whether the participants understand the material and to keep them tuned in to the lesson.

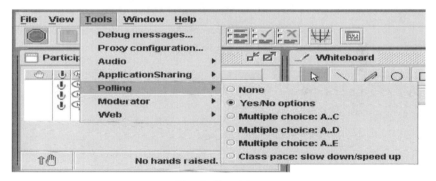

vClass Polling Menu

- Use surveys to transition to a new topic by asking questions about the new topic and then commenting on the results.
- Create icebreakers and introductory exercises by polling the audience.
- Share results with the class to foster a sense of community.
- Asking participants to provide feedback can be a good reengagement technique if the audience is not participating.

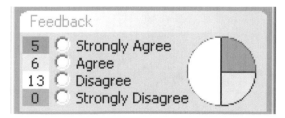

Instructor Feedback Results in LearnLinc

TABLE 1.1.   Common Synchronous Features and Their Uses, Cont'd.

- Anonymous feedback allows participants to be honest without worrying about repercussions.
- If you are not comfortable with receiving and responding to continual feedback, you might introduce this feature slowly.

CONSIDERATIONS
- What survey and/or polling tools are available with the platform?
- Can the results be shared with the class?
- Can questions be created spontaneously?
- Is the feedback anonymous/confidential?

SYNCHRONOUS FEATURE: TESTING/EVALUATION

This feature allows the trainer to conduct pre-session and post-session assessments and tests, the results of which can be automatically tabulated and saved.

USES
- Use this feature to assess your participants' comprehension and retention.
- If these built-in solutions aren't robust enough, savvy users can create assessments in HTML and post them to participants using the application window. Or participants can be instructed to use commercial web-based assessment tools like QuestionMark™ (www.questionmark.com) and Zoomerang™ (www.zoomerang.com).

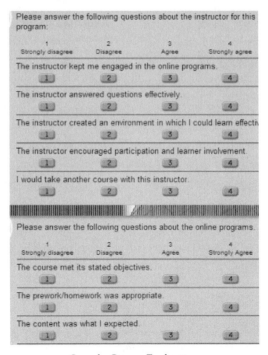

Sample Course Evaluation

TABLE 1.1. Common Synchronous Features and Their Uses, Cont'd.

CONSIDERATIONS

• How are evaluation and testing results reported?

• How are results saved?

SYNCHRONOUS FEATURE: LIVE VIDEO

One-way or two-way video is offered by more sophisticated synchronous packages.

This is a very technology-intensive feature, which often limits its use to participants using broadband connections. (An exception is the use of streaming media in one-way video configurations, which can be fed to participants with connections as slow as 56 Kbps.)

Some platforms recognize users with dial-up connections and automatically suppress video to those users or send out fewer "frames per second."

USES

• You can use the video to look directly into the camera for live Q&A sessions.

• Using live video throughout a session can be very distracting; you should use it judiciously. If face-to-face interactions are critical, consider using a traditional classroom approach instead. Or record video and distribute before the session using the Internet, videotape, or CD-ROM.

LearnLinc's Video Viewer

TABLE 1.1.   Common Synchronous Features and Their Uses, Cont'd.

CONSIDERATIONS

• What are the hardware and software requirements for live video?

SYNCHRONOUS FEATURE: DISCUSSION BOARDS

A discussion board is an asynchronous feature that allows participants to post messages and replies to messages by topic. Discussion boards are different from chat in that they are not real-time.

While a discussion board is an asynchronous feature, it is often bundled with synchronous packages.

If your software does not have a discussion board, you can consider a third-party product like Blackboard™ (www.blackboard.com) or WebCT™ (www.webtct.com).

USES

• Use discussion boards to post class information, FAQs, pre-session or post-session assignments, subject-matter expert insights, or other information relevant to the synchronous session.

⌐ 90. Q1.1. How does systematic design differ from other methods used to design instruction (e.g., SME approach)?
⌐ 93. Q1.1. How does systematic design differ from other methods used to design instruction (e.g., SME approach)?
⌐ 73. Q1.1. How does systematic design differ from other methods used to design instruction (e.g., SME approach)?
⌐ 75. Q1.1. How does systematic design differ from other methods used to design instruction (e.g., SME approach)?
⌐ 25. Updated tips for formulating your response
▼⌐ 27. Romano's initial post
   ⌐ 53. Romano's initial post
   ⌐ 77. Romano's initial post
   ⌐ 95. Romano's initial post
▼⌐ 33. Re: Q1.1 How does systematic design differ ....
   ⌐ 54. Re: Q1.1 How does systematic design differ ....

Sample Threaded Discussion

• For multi-session classes, encourage participants to use the discussion boards for knowledge sharing and community building. You'll need to stay involved to make sure this is successful.

• Often, classes that include such asynchronous activities as discussion boards and short synchronous online sessions are more effective than using just one delivery method.

CONSIDERATIONS

• Are discussion boards available during class?

SYNCHRONOUS FEATURE: APPLICATION SHARING

This feature allows the trainer to share software applications (such as spreadsheets) with participants.

TABLE 1.1.   Common Synchronous Features and Their Uses, Cont'd.

There are many varieties of this feature, ranging from "view only" on the participants' side to allowing participants to actually interact with applications shared by the trainer or by other participants.

USES

- Use application sharing to demonstrate software features.

- Small groups can collaborate by sharing common office software packages.

- Individuals can walk through software applications with which they are having difficulty.

- Participants can use shared applications in breakout rooms. There, you can also assist individuals with assigned exercises.

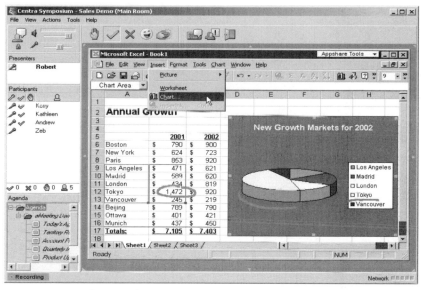

Application Sharing in Centra Symposium (Student View)

CONSIDERATIONS

- What types of applications can be shared?
- What are the bandwidth requirements for application sharing?
- Can participants interact with the application or just view it?

SYNCHRONOUS FEATURE: SYNCHRONIZED WEB BROWSING

This feature allows the trainer or participants to bring the class to an Internet site or corporate intranet.

Often, you can use this feature to run short, self-paced exercises as part of a synchronous session.

TABLE 1.1. Common Synchronous Features and Their Uses, Cont'd.

USES

- Instead of recreating content that already exists, you can use the Internet or corporate intranet as a content source.
- Participants can share related content by your leading the class to a website.
- Independent exercises can be initiated for the entire group—including web-enabled, self-paced exercises created in multimedia applications.
- Last-minute content can be added to an existing program by placing it on the web.

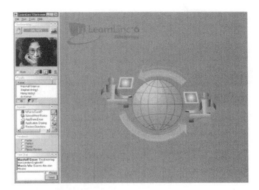

LearnLinc's Synchronized Web Browser

CONSIDERATIONS

- Can a participant bring the class to a website?
- Can bookmarks be created prior to class to speed navigation?
- Does this feature require a specific browser?
- Are hyperlinks available to individual participants?

SYNCHRONOUS FEATURE: RECORD AND PLAYBACK

This feature allows individuals to record synchronous events and play them back later.

Often, parts of recordings can be edited into synchronous sessions or entire recordings can be "cleaned up" for on-demand viewing.

This feature helps individuals who miss sessions and allows for quick creation of asynchronous training content.

USES

- You can use the record/playback feature to practice and review the participants' and the trainer's performances.

TABLE 1.1.   Common Synchronous Features and Their Uses, Cont'd.

- You can preview existing programs to review content.
- Participants can use recordings to preview or review course materials.
- Participants who miss one session of a multi-session program need not miss the content.
- This is a relatively inexpensive way to create self-paced, "videotaped" classes.
- This feature is a very efficient way to prep new trainers.
- Be sure to tell participants they are being recorded! Often, there is an indicator on the screen to act as a reminder.

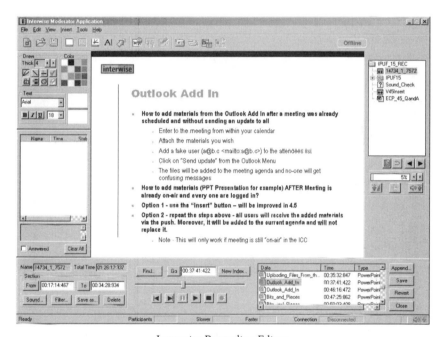

Interwise Recording Editor

CONSIDERATIONS

- Is special software required to view the recordings?
- Can recordings be viewed while not connected to the Internet?
- Can trainers stop the recorder and start it up again in the same session?

SYNCHRONOUS FEATURE: ASSISTANT TRAINER

Feature that allows a second individual to assist the trainer with some of the facilitation tasks. Some programs allow for multiple assistants.

TABLE 1.1.   Common Synchronous Features and Their Uses, Cont'd.

Assistant trainers do not need to be in the same location as the trainer, but they can still use an "instructor" version of the synchronous application to conduct various tasks—from dealing with technical support issues to helping with the content.

USES

- If your class requires a subject-matter expert in the delivery, he or she can help in the assistant trainer role by answering questions and providing lecture assistance.

- The assistant trainer role is perfect for a trainer-in-training. The assistant trainer can interact as a participant and assist you at the same time.

- If you have a special guest trainer who doesn't know how to manage the synchronous technology, you can manage the technology while the guest, acting as the assistant, leads the discussion.

In vClass the Assistant Trainer Is Identified by the Word "Moderator"

CONSIDERATIONS

- What can a lead trainer do that an assistant trainer cannot do (create breakout rooms, launch applications, and so forth)?

- Do assistants need to be identified ahead of time, or can individuals be "promoted" during the live event?

SYNCHRONOUS FEATURE: CONTENT WINDOWS

Content windows are used to display content in HTML, PowerPoint® or other web-ready media.

TABLE 1.1.   Common Synchronous Features and Their Uses, Cont'd.

PowerPoint is the most popular content creation tool. When the slides are loaded into some synchronous platforms, the slides may become backgrounds for whiteboards.

USES

- Remember that synchronous classrooms are a very visual medium. What you show in the content windows needs to be relevant and engaging.

- Don't plan to read the content on your screen verbatim. If that's the nature of the content, consider an asynchronous or self-paced delivery instead.

- Use multimedia when it makes sense—not just because you can. Remember that every time you add a new technology, you are also adding a potential technical obstacle.

- Some software packages allow you to use pre-created content as whiteboard backgrounds. This can be a very effective engagement tool.

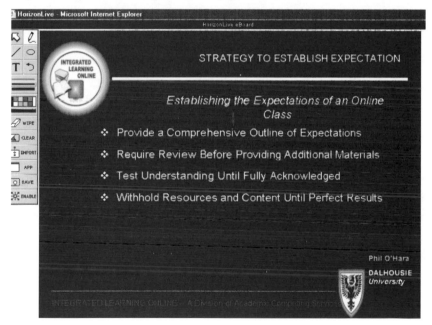

HorizonLive's Content Window "eBoard"

CONSIDERATIONS

- Can content be added during the live event?
- How are plug-ins managed?
- What file formats can be used?
- Are web and/or PowerPoint animations viewable?
- Can you write on top of animated content?

QUESTIONS ABOUT THIS CHAPTER:

IDEAS AND APPLICATIONS:

2

Facilitating in the Synchronous Classroom

Think back to the first time you stood up in front of a classroom and presented to a group of people. Can you remember the training you had to prepare for that event? Maybe you enrolled in an "Effective Presentations" or a "Train the Trainer" program. Perhaps you shadowed a more experienced trainer. You certainly relied on your experience as a participant. Let's face it; we've all been attending traditional classroom sessions since we were children. We understand the need to make eye contact and interpret body language. We did not need a class to learn that you use markers to write on flip charts. It was not a reach to figure out that someone with a puzzled look might not be keeping up with the class. And if someone fell asleep during your lecture? Well, you probably knew what that meant as well.

Now think about why you became a trainer. Did you like being in front of a group of people? Were you a subject-matter expert who was able to present ideas very effectively? Did you like watching the proverbial light bulb go off over a participant's head?

When you think about your answers to these questions, it is easy to see why many trainers (maybe even you!) are hesitant about teaching in the synchronous classroom. We've asked you to lead in an environment where you have not mastered the skill of being a participant. We've taken away physical proximity. The language of eye contact and body movements, which we have spent so much of our lives learning to interpret, is no longer applicable.

So what's a trainer to do?

This chapter will help you answer that question. We will discuss the profile of an effective synchronous trainer, the components of a synchronous trainer's workstation, the logistics of working with a producer, and other items that will help you find success in the synchronous classroom.

Profile of an Effective Synchrononous Trainer

Wanted:

Synchronous Trainer. Experienced training professional with five years working with synchronous training methods. Must be able to create HTML, PowerPoint®, and use various authoring tools in order to create engaging media. Master's in Educational Technology preferred.

Does this description look familiar? Does it look like you or anyone you know? Probably not—at least not yet. Synchronously delivered web-based training has not been a viable delivery method for very long; trainers have just recently started to create best practices.

Learning technologies are forcing many trainers into situations that they never expected when they signed up to be trainers. Stand-up presentation skills, the ability to apply adult learning principles in a practical manner, and subject-matter expertise were the primary qualifications for the job. More and more often, trainers are finding that these skills are not enough. Technical understanding and troubleshooting techniques have become requirements.

In order to bring the ideal talent into organizations, we need to identify people who can succeed as synchronous trainers. How do you know if you can succeed? While there is no guaranteed formula for success, there are a few characteristics that will help.

The trainer leads the synchronous event by providing instruction in real time. It is the trainer's responsibility to do the following:

- *Direct the learning.* The trainer must watch the time and ensure that the instructional objectives for the session are met.

- *Control the learning environment.* A lot can happen at once. If participants are all trying to talk at the same time, or having too many unrelated chat conversations, or not participating enough, the trainer must find ways to bring everyone back into the fold and prevent confusion.

- *Communicate with the participants.* It is easy to overlook participants who are not interacting with the class. The trainer must pay attention and be sure that everyone is invited to be involved and encouraged to participate.

- *Predict participants' needs.* New synchronous participants may need more time to complete activities because of their lack of familiarity with the collaboration tools. Long lectures may have to be interspersed with breaks or hands-on activities to break up the monotony. Trainers must stay tuned-in to maintain the comfort level and keep participants engaged.

- *Encourage interaction.* It is easy for synchronous training to become all about the trainer and a passive experience for the participants. Without "something to do" every three to five minutes, participants can easily become disengaged.

> ▶ "Something to do" could mean participate in a chat exercise, answer questions, take a quiz . . . anything that keeps participants involved. Be sure that it is more than just busy work. The activity should support the instruction.

As you can see, in many ways, the job description for the synchronous trainer is the same as that for a traditional classroom trainer. In addition to the skills listed above, a successful synchronous trainer:

- *Is collaborative.* The synchronous classroom is not the place for the "sage-on-the-stage" type of trainer. In order to encourage learning and keep the participants engaged, you need to maintain an active part in the process.

- *Is an advocate of the synchronous classroom.* Project a positive attitude before, during, and after the event. If you do not believe that your participants can learn in this environment, your participants and peers will not believe it either.

- *Is a broadcaster.* Radio broadcasters keep their energy up and speak to their audiences conversationally. They do not need to see the audience to interact with it. Synchronous trainers also must keep their voices up and attitudes positive, no matter how many participants are listening. Like a radio broadcaster, you must address the individuals in the group and make your comments personal.

- *Has a dynamic voice.* The next time you are watching a very dynamic and effective speaker, close your eyes. Is the message as effective when you can't see the speaker? If not, that person might need some voice coaching before becoming a synchronous trainer.

- *Is flexible.* Lots of last-minute, unanticipated problems can occur when working remotely via web technology. Synchronous trainers must be able to maintain the course flow and manage high-stress situations with grace.

- *Thrives under stress.* A new recruit once shared that synchronous training was "not for the faint of heart." Her first synchronous training experience resulted in a host of problems: She lost her connection to the Internet, her supervisor decided to log in "just to check in," her class ran thirty minutes late, and she lost half of her participants to technical problems. (She couldn't wait to do it again!)

- *Is a multi-tasker.* In the virtual world, trainers must handle many things at the same time. It is important for them to feel comfortable managing multiple tasks simultaneously.

- *Is a participant first.* Classroom trainers know what it's like to learn in a traditional setting. They have been doing it all of their lives. Most new online trainers, on the other hand, have not participated in live online programs before (except, potentially, programs designed to teach them the software). Find a class and immerse yourself in the participant experience. How does the "dead air" make you feel? What do you do when the technology breaks down? What makes an exercise effective? You cannot anticipate the reactions of your participants unless you have "walked a mile in their shoes."

Once you decide you want to be a synchronous trainer, practice as much as possible. You must practice to learn the technology, and you must practice to learn how to deliver your content through the medium. You will find that even the most familiar classroom content will have to be delivered differently in the synchronous environment.

For many reasons, some trainers will decide that they do not want to pursue teaching synchronously. We will always need exceptional classroom trainers to support the more traditional methods of delivery, so don't try to force this issue if you decide, after some experimentation, that synchronous training is not for you. If you do not enjoy the experience, your participants will not enjoy the full benefits of the learning environment.

The Synchronous Trainer's Workstation

Just as in traditional classroom training, it is important that you have a place in which you can effectively facilitate. Make sure you are in an environment that is conducive to online training.

An ideal environment includes the following:

- A *private, soundproof room.* You don't want to be disturbed by the work going on around you. And you don't want to disturb your colleagues. Imagine listening to one side of a conference call for hours at a time!

▶ If you are delivering training from your home, you have a different set of issues. I have learned to hang a sign on my front
door telling people that even though I am obviously at home I
am not going to answer the door no matter how many times
they knock! If you have family at home, make sure children are
fed and occupied. You will not be able to help them during
the class.

- A *nearby restroom*. Your breaks will only be about ten minutes
  long–and you can't be late coming back.

- A *high-speed Internet connection*. High-speed generally means
  faster than dial-up modems. The faster the connection with
  the Internet, the better the experience will be for everyone
  because audio and visuals will transmit quickly. When slower
  connections are used, there may be noticeable lags in the time
  it takes data (audio or video) to go back and forth between
  the trainer and participants. (Note that most synchronous
  platforms work quite well at dial-up connection speeds—they
  just work BETTER at higher connection speeds.)

- A *telephone*. You'll need to be able to contact missing participants, technical support, and your producer. If you are using a
  dial-up modem for your connection, you will want two phone
  lines. It is fine to depend on a mobile phone for this—just
  make sure you have a strong phone signal and that the phone
  will not run out of battery power during the event. You should
  probably keep it plugged in.

- *Number for live technical support*. While technical support does
  not need to be on call or logged in for the entire event, you
  need to know whom to call if the server goes down and stays
  down. Ensure that the technical support team knows the
  schedule of your classes. Many technical support organizations post email notices when they anticipate interruptions
  of service of any kind (for example, while they are upgrading

computer hardware or software). Ask to be added to this distribution list so you know when it might affect your events.

- A *participant list*. You should have a printed contact list of participants and event support contacts with you at every program. If the worst happens and your computer stops working, you can at least call your participants to let them know what is going on. It will also help you to take attendance during the class.

- A *"Do Not Disturb" sign*. On the sign, you might indicate the time class is scheduled to be over as well. This way, people will know when they can reach you. Make sure those around you respect this sign. I've had colleagues stick their heads in while I am teaching to ask how the class is going. When I point out the sign, they inevitably say that they didn't think it applied to them.

- A *powerful computer*. This should be a desktop computer with a high-resolution screen, 128 Megs RAM, updated browsers, the most up-to-date version of the necessary software and courseware, and excellent microphones and speakers or headsets. If you don't know what these terms mean or how powerful your computer is, talk to someone who does know, like your technical support help desk. When you speak with technical support, consider asking them about courses that will help you become more fluent in computer terminology and functionality. This way you can be prepared when a synchronous participant asks you questions like, "How do I adjust the audio on my headset?"

- An *additional computer*. Having an additional computer allows you to view the participant environment. This can be especially helpful during sessions that incorporate application sharing and web browsing. You can make sure that the "dummy" participant on your extra computer is exactly where you are (the dummy should be looking at the screen in the exact same way that you are) before you move on (see sample on page 36).

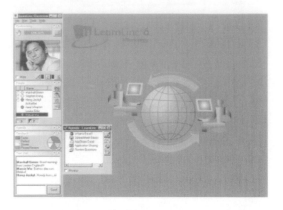

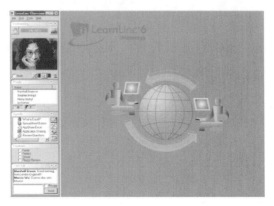

LearnLine Instructor and Student View

- *A studio microphone and speakers.* When I teach, I often like to have a wireless microphone or a microphone in a stand in-stead of a headset attached to the computer. This allows me to walk around, make gestures, and keep my energy up. Being tied to the computer can make a trainer lethargic. I have found, though, that when I use this type of microphone, I need to plug it into a different input hole than the one I would use for a headset microphone. This will probably vary depending on the PC you are using; just remember that differ-ent equipment works differently, so be sure to test your input device and make note of what you need to adjust in order to maximize performance. (For more on using non-standard audio devices, see Chapter 5 on Managing the Technology.)

- A *computer drawing tablet*. A drawing tablet is a piece of computer hardware that lies flat on your desk. It is often the size of a piece of paper. It comes with an "electronic pen" or stylus. Instead of trying to "draw" on the whiteboard using a computer mouse, you can use the tablet and stylus. Because this replicates writing, you can create a much more realistic, and readable, visual for your participants than you would be drawing with a mouse. This is not always a common piece of equipment, so ask your technical support contact how you can determine what tablet may be right for you.

- A *pitcher of water*. A synchronous trainer needs to create his own energy and stay active. Water (or your beverage of choice) can keep you energized. If you are using a headset-type microphone, you'll probably want to keep some drinking straws on hand. Synchronous trainers often move the microphone out of the way in order to take a sip and forget to move it back when they start talking again.

The Producer

You might hear the producer referred to as the "assistant instructor" or as the "assistant trainer." This role is very specific to the synchronous classroom. It is also the most controversial role on the team. While it is very true that successful events can be run without a producer, my experience has convinced me that if you want a "high-touch" program with rich interactions and minimal technical interruptions, the help of a producer is essential.

The producer assists the trainer by acting as an extra pair of hands during a synchronous event. The producer does not need to be in the same physical location as the trainer. In addition to handling training responsibilities, the producer handles technical support so the trainer can focus on the instruction. Using a producer practically eliminates the need for live event technical support.

Working with a Producer

Many factors influence when and how to use a producer:

- *Logistical.* Is another person available to act as a producer? Does the budget allow for this person?
- *Technical.* Does your software platform support an "assistant" of some sort? If not, what can someone logged in as a participant do to assist?
- *Instructional.* Do the design and desired outcomes require an assistant?
- *Personal.* Do you find yourself thinking, "I don't use an assistant in the traditional classroom so why do I need one now?"

Additionally, you must consider your own expectations. Do you want the quality of your synchronous training to meet or exceed the standards you have set for your classroom training? If the answer to that question is "no" and your expectations for synchronous training results are not as strenuous, you may forgo the producer and use a more lecture or auditorium-type approach.

I encourage you to experiment with this role before making your final determination. You may decide that some courses, audiences, or trainers require an extra set of hands.

"One Is the Loneliest Number"

Trainers tend to be social people. We like to share stories, commiserate, and generally interact with other people. Often, departments in organizations select one person to be the synchronous trainer for the group. This type of isolation can make a challenging task even more difficult—there is no one who understands what the trainer is experiencing and no one to turn to for advice. But if a producer is used, the trainer and producer can work together to improve the learning experience for the participants. If both parties are qualified to deliver the content, you effectively have two producers and two trainers—able to back one another up.

"An Extra Pair of Hands"

There are countless benefits to working with a producer, but my team likes to sum it up this way:

> When you lose eye contact you need an extra set of hands to compensate!!!!

Usually, the producer assumes many of the technical responsibilities during a synchronous event. For instance, the producer can handle participants' technical problems, set up breakout rooms, and monitor the chat area.

The producer is also essential for maintaining a high level of interaction with participants. For example, the producer might help make the slides more dynamic by using the whiteboard tools to highlight and add material. The producer can also help manage breakout rooms and assist participants with assignments.

If you discover that you have different levels of participant experience in a session, a producer with a solid grasp of the content can assist by managing a chat exercise with the more experienced participants while you continue a lecture with the less experienced participants. This is a great technique when you are concerned that the more advanced participants may lose interest and log out early—especially when there is information more relevant to them later in the program.

I have found that, while the role of producer is always helpful, it becomes more critical when I want to facilitate a very "high-touch" class with eight or more participants.

Production Tasks

Following is a list of typical production tasks:

- *Handle technical questions and problems.* Any major technical
  problems should have been identified and fixed long before
  the synchronous training, but even prepared participants can
  run into problems during a live event. A trainer who tries to
  fix the problems can lose valuable class time. Instead, give participants the producer's phone number so he or she can manage any technical support issues that arise. The producer can
  assess whether the participant can return to class or whether
  another level of technical support is required.

- *Respond to messages and manage chat.* Many trainers limit the
  use of the chat and message features because they find it impossible to respond while also facilitating a class. However,
  crucial interaction can occur in the chat and message areas.
  For example, five participants suddenly sending questions at
  the same time can be a sign that participants have missed a
  key point. People chatting off-topic may mean that the current activity is not engaging enough. People chatting on-topic
  may have something important to add to the conversation.
  The producer can watch for all of these signals, answer questions, and alert the trainer when he or she needs to become
  involved.

- *Launch surveys, breakout rooms, and shared applications.* While
  the trainer is engaged with participants, the producer should
  ensure that all of the exercises that require technology setup
  are in queue and ready to launch as soon as the trainer is ready
  for them. This minimizes "dead air" and makes the program
  move quickly.

- *Scribe on the whiteboard.* Activity on the whiteboard, including
  scribing a participant's comments, writing down important
  points, and capturing instructions, makes the program more
  visually engaging and helps participants focus. The producer
  can scribe while the trainer is otherwise engaged.

- *Warm up the participants before class begins.* While participants are logging on, the producer can verify that the technology is working, answer navigation questions, and facilitate warm-up exercises. When the trainer starts speaking or typing, participants know class has begun.

The producer can become very busy in a high-touch collaborative event! Here are some other things a producer can do to assist:

- Assign speaking privileges to participants as they join the class and ask them each to say "Hello."
- Help participants adjust their audio levels.
- Write the technical support number on the whiteboard.
- Call participants who have not logged on to class; assist with technical issues.
- Engage participants in the chat area who have more experience with the content or seem to be bored.
- Remind the trainer when a participant has not interacted for ten minutes or more.
- Track timing and keep the trainer on schedule.
- Use the whiteboard tools to draw attention to each bulleted item as the trainer mentions it.
- Type instructions on the whiteboard.
- Manage half of the breakout rooms by assisting the participants with the exercise.
- Launch the course evaluation.
- Start/stop recording and publish the session.

Besides assisting trainers in live events, there are several other advantages to having a producer:

- You can treat the producer role as a method of training new synchronous trainers. The producer can serve as a co-trainer, gain mastery of the content, and observe participants while assisting the trainer with "traditional" production tasks.

- As synchronous technology becomes more popular in your organization, you will see the demand for synchronous meetings, subject-matter expert forums, and announcements arise. You can use your trained producers as meeting facilitators to manage and facilitate these events. You may find that once word gets around, your production team will become a commodity!

Team-Teaching Tips

Here are some tips for making the trainer/producer model work for you:

- Create a leader guide that specifically outlines production tasks. For example, include instructions for writing on the whiteboard, conducting warm-up exercises, and pasting text into the chat area. The guide should be very specific and cover the "when" and the "why" in addition to the "what." Format the guide so that the production tasks can be quickly identified to be better prepared for times when a producer is not available. Read over the lists of tasks to make informed decisions about which items you can manage on your own and which need to be modified in the absence of a second pair of hands. (More detail about leader guides is provided later in this chapter.)

- Meet at least a week ahead of time to walk through and discuss the exercises. This meeting is best held in a synchronous format so that the you and the producer can plan exactly how things are going to work. It will also allow the producer, who may not be a content expert, to become familiar with the content. During this walk-through, lay out how the producer should respond to content questions in the chat area.

- Establish emergency protocols. What happens if you drop offline and the producer is left with a room full of participants? Decide ahead of time. The producer should know whether to call for a break or to ask participants to complete an exercise, such as typing into chat all of the questions they have for you when you return. Or short self-paced exercises can be included in course workbooks so that the producer can direct people to them while they're waiting for you to return.

- Establish course ground rules. The producer needs to know how to respond to participants who get to class late or leave early. For example, if someone logs on twenty minutes into a program, should the producer tell him or her that class has already started and provide a schedule for future offerings?

- Ensure that the producer has all participant and leader materials. This will make it easier for him or her to support both you and the participants.

- Rehearse in a realistic environment. Consider whether you, the producer, or participants will be logging on with dial-up modems and/or behind firewalls. If you and the producer will be at remote locations during the live event, then the rehearsal should be conducted that way as well.

- Create an environment of trust. The trainer/producer relationship should represent a true team. For example, if the producer suggests that you take a moment to review the questions in the chat area, you must trust that issues there are worth considering.

- Debrief the experience. After the live event, share notes about what went well and what needs to be changed. Make sure you document lessons learned for different trainer/ producer pairs who may tackle your class in the future.

- Have the producer log on as the "lead" trainer if your software platform provides more technical functionality for a "lead" trainer than for an "assistant" trainer. This way, the producer can handle technical tasks like setting up breakout rooms while you focus on teaching.

- Work as a team. You and the producer should be able to give each other advice and direction throughout a live event without causing distractions or creating anxiety. As a team, you should not second-guess one another.

Juggling Everything on Your Own

No matter how convincing the arguments are for using a producer, some trainers will not have that luxury. They will need to jump right in and manage events on their own. If this is the case with you, take an objective look at the planned exercises and make decisions about how realistic it is that they can be facilitated by one person. Practice becomes even more important. You need to be very comfortable with the technology before teaching.

I suggest using a producer early in your synchronous training initiatives. This environment is new to everyone, and it is critical to have initial successes in order to prove the long-term viability of the delivery method. When you are learning a new skill, four hands are better than two!

Leader Guides for Trainer/Producer Collaboration

The purpose of a leader guide in a traditional setting is to direct action and dialog during a specified period of time. Leader guides help to ensure that every class is uniform, keep the agenda on track, provide confidence for new trainers, and allow a substitute trainer to get up to speed quickly.

Leader guides are just as important in the synchronous environment as they are in a traditional training environment. Potentially, more so. Synchronous leader guides can contain technical instructions for both the trainer and the producer that ensure that synchronous collaboration tools are used smoothly and with impact.

An unexpected benefit of the synchronous environment is that the trainer and producer can use the leader guide openly during the event. Since participants cannot see them, they do not need to know that the trainer and producer are referring to a guide. This does not alleviate the need for practice and rehearsal, but it does reduce some of the pressure associated with new programs.

The following figures illustrate the basic structure of the leader guides I use to facilitate synchronous events. The first is a mockup version of the page layout, and the second shows some production tasks that require timing-coordination between the producer and the trainer.

Figure 2.1 shows a simplified version of a leader guide layout. Notice that the production tasks and facilitation tasks are on separate, but adjacent, pages. (There are many ways to design the guide, but it is critical that trainer and producer tasks support one another.)

This format serves several purposes:

- Both the producer and the trainer see a thumbnail of the slide.
- The trainer is not distracted by the producer's tasks (and vice versa).
- The trainer can see what the producer is doing at a glance (and vice versa).
- If the trainer does not have the luxury of using a producer, he or she can determine which exercises can be managed independently and which need to be adjusted.

On each page of the leader guide, the tasks are displayed in chronological order. And, for the most part, timing between the producer and the trainer is either obvious or irrelevant. That is, some tasks must necessarily occur before others (launching the slide, for example). And some tasks—like responding to chat notes—are not dependent on any other actions. But there are cases when the timing must be more coordinated. For example, a trainer might ask a series of questions of participants. The correct answers are available to the producer in a word document. However, since participants are volunteering the answers, the producer should not paste the material until the answer has been revealed. The trainer and producer must target and review these timing situations prior to the synchronous event. (Leader guides are discussed in more detail in Chapter 4, Synchronous Classroom Management.)

FIGURE 2.1 Sample Page Mockup.

Left Facing Page

Right Facing Page

Timing: Not to exceed 5 minutes

Production Tasks	Facilitation Tasks
Capture participants' remarks on the whiteboard. **Identify** participants by writing their names next to their remarks. Use a **different color** for each participant.	**Say:** What did you learn during this online session that surprised you? **Call** on individuals one at a time. Make sure that everyone has the opportunity to participate.
	After each participant has had an opportunity to contribute, quickly debrief and summarize the remarks.

QUESTIONS ABOUT THIS CHAPTER:

IDEAS AND APPLICATIONS:

3

Communicating in the Synchronous Classroom

The most frequent question I receive goes something like this:

> In a traditional classroom, 90 percent of an instructor's credibility comes from his or her physical presence. So how do you create credibility and keep people engaged when you have no physical presence, hand gestures, or eye contact?

Online synchronous instruction is a different medium with vastly different rules and considerations than traditional classroom training. You cannot give a nod of reassurance or a smile of approval. You no longer have the advantages of eye contact and body language; you have to rely on very subtle cues from your participants instead. Now your visual aids (slides and media) and your voice are your only means of communicating, so it is essential that you use both your visuals and your voice to convey enthusiasm and a high energy level to your participants.

Using Visuals

According to the "Ten Commandments of Presentations," published by the *Harvard Management Communication Letter*, "An enormous number of businesspeople watch an even greater number of slides day in and day out because speakers have half-learned a dubious wisdom that there are visual learners out there and that a large number of slides will help them learn. . . . Yes, those visual learners like pictures. They also like good metaphors, videos, broad overviews, and enthusiastic gestures. What they don't like is one slide after another paced with words."

In the synchronous classroom the trainer could literally be a continent away from a participant. When you remove the eye contact between trainer and participant, an abundance of bulleted slides becomes even less effective. Counteract that by using images to create a presentation theme. When introducing a concept for the first time, create an icon to represent that idea. When you must use bullet points, make them engaging. You can use a question mark as a bullet when you ask questions and an exclamation point as a bullet to make strong points. Use road signs, automobiles, office supplies, fruit—anything to keep your participants peering at the screen and not out the window.

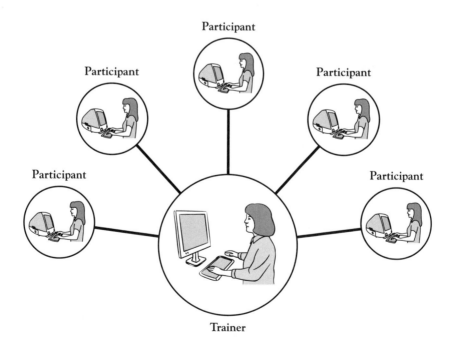

Your media and slides are the major focal points of the synchronous event. The 480 x 640 pixel area (a common content area size) provided by software platforms is the only possible place for visual interaction. This space has, in essence, replaced your body language, so make sure you take advantage of it. Some ways to do that include making the screen change, using a combination of graphics and photos, changing fonts and colors, and using a combination of media types. Every time the screen changes, you have a new opportunity to re-engage your participants. As the screens advance, the participant's mind signals, "Watch-out—something important might be coming."

Here are some general tips for your slides:

- *Don't create slides that you plan to read verbatim.* They are boring, and participants can read ahead quickly, then tune you out before you finish the slide. Instead use visuals with just headers and/or key words. Use whiteboard tools or chat to add additional written information where appropriate.

- *Use multimedia when it makes sense, not just because you can.* Multimedia additions can be engaging and memorable when they are used appropriately, but too many bells and whistles can distract from your instruction. Remember that every time you add a new technology, you are also adding a potential technical obstacle.

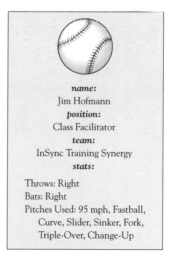

name:
Jim Hofmann
position:
Class Facilitator
team:
InSync Training Synergy
stats:
Throws: Right
Bats: Right
Pitches Used: 95 mph, Fastball,
Curve, Slider, Sinker, Fork,
Triple-Over, Change-Up

This trainer introduction page was used during a class with a baseball theme. All key "players" in this class had a baseball card to identify them.

- *Vary your slides*. Slide after slide with the same look and feel will not keep your participants' attention for long. Throw in some variations to keep the presentation interesting and engaging. Using your own handwriting on the slides can be effective; it humanizes the instruction and minimizes the feeling of distance between you and your participants.

- *Collaborate rather than lecture*. Don't use your slides as your primary method of communicating content. Ask participants to brainstorm ideas. Create exercises using chat and whiteboard technologies. Incorporate reading assignments and checklists into your participant guides.

Using Your Voice

In the synchronous environment, your voice is your most essential instructional tool. Here are some tips for using it effectively:

- *Vary your intonations*. Nobody likes to listen to a monotonous voice, even when there are many things to look at. Remember that, when your voice is the star of the show, it's crucial that you make it as interesting as possible. You might also draw on other voices to help you out—that of your producer, perhaps, or the participants as they read onscreen text for you. You'll be amazed how something as simple as a new voice can re-engage your participants.

- *Don't over-project*. While you want your voice to be interesting, be sure that the volume and other aspects of your delivery remain conversational.

- *Be positive and use humor*. Remember—if you are emitting signals of anxiety, your participants will detect it. When you insert humor, you won't hear your audience laughing (or groaning) so you need to imagine it. You might even say something like, "I know that was the funniest thing you heard this week. Feel free to use it." As in any training situation, be selective about the humor you employ; while it can break the ice or lighten the mood, you want to be sure not to offend any participants.

- *Smile and use hand gestures.* Participants can "hear" it. Although your participants cannot see you, using natural gestures will improve your intonation and delivery. You may not want to use a headset that physically restricts you to the computer; it might stifle your presentations.

    ▶ The use of hand gestures and facial expressions when you are seemingly talking to yourself might invite some strange looks. This is another good reason to teach from a private space.

- *Be careful not to sound too scripted.* As a synchronous trainer, you can get away with reading scripts right from your document. Don't take this as permission not to prepare—if your delivery sounds too scripted, you might lose your participants' attention. Change your intonations and pace, and make sure you emphasize appropriate words and phrases. Also, if your eyes are on the script, they are not on the classroom. You may miss important feedback.

Language Tips

Soon after I began to teach synchronously, I realized that I had to make some adjustments to my language in order to elicit the responses I desired. Here are some lessons learned:

- *Call on participants by name.* In a traditional classroom, trainers often rely on physical cues to determine understanding and ask questions. In the synchronous classroom, we don't have that luxury. When participants know they might be called on at any time, they pay more attention. I tell them ahead of time that I will call on them to answer questions, and I insist on some level of participation. I can always see the list of participants logged into the class, and I try to engage those I have not heard from in a while.

- *Learn new ways to ask questions.* There are some natural ways to get feedback in a traditional classroom. For example, when a trainer asks, "Any questions?" he or she looks around the room and gauges body language. If there is a question, it is often just called out at that point. You would think that the verbal interplay would work the same way online, but there are some subtle differences. In a synchronous classroom, what should a participant do when asked, "Any questions?" Is the proper response clicking "Yes," raising a virtual hand, or pasting the question in the chat area? If there are no questions, is the proper response to do nothing or to click the "No" button? It is less confusing to say, "Raise your hand if you have a question" or "Send your questions in the chat area." There are many other examples. If you say, "Click 'Yes' if you are ready to move on," how should participants who are not ready respond? Should they click "No," raise their hands, or do nothing? You'll soon discover the best ways to ask questions.

- *Don't emphasize the technology with your language.* It's a natural inclination when teaching synchronously to underscore every technical action. You might say, for instance, "Becky, I see that you have your hand raised" or "Now I'm going to clear the whiteboard." Such comments are unnatural; you certainly wouldn't announce such things in a traditional classroom. Additionally, they don't add any instructional value to the course. It will probably take practice and some effort, but try to avoid drawing attention to the technology. It is also common to hear trainers apologize for obstacles like bandwidth issues and technology problems. While you don't want to ignore real issues, repetitive apologies for small glitches reinforce the technology and not the learning.

- *Time-release your instructions.* Through a lot of trial and error, my team discovered this simple truth: Don't overload your participants with too many instructions at once. This is especially true for small-group or independent activities. Participants, especially those new to the synchronous classroom, have a difficult time retaining a list of tasks. Provide duplicate instructions in their workbooks, and have them locate these instructions before you send them off to work on their own. Also, reinforce how participants can contact you (usually the chat function) in case they have questions while they are working independently.

- *Don't talk too much.* Your participants' attention is difficult to capture and even more difficult to keep. Use short "lecturettes" and break them up with meaningful interactions. My general rule of thumb is that if I've been talking for more than three or four minutes, I've been talking too long.

ADVANCED TIP

In general, trainers and participants use Internet audio by holding down a key while they are speaking. Many synchronous classroom vendors offer a "Push to Talk" button, which allows the speaker to activate the microphone and speak without holding down any keys. When they have finished speaking, they deactivate the microphone. While sometimes this feature is necessary (for example, while using the application-sharing feature), I avoid using the "Push to Talk" feature when I can. A colleague shared that he uses "Push to Talk" because his finger gets tired from holding down the assigned key while he is lecturing. My response: If your finger is getting tired, that's a signal to stop talking and initiate some interaction!

Gauging Participation

Because synchronous participants are not under the watchful eye of the trainer, I wonder: What are they doing while a trainer is happily lecturing away from a remote location? I asked participants about some of the things they have done while in synchronous classes. Here is a sampling of their responses:

- Listening to the lecture and taking notes (I'm glad SOME people answered this way).
- Answering email messages.
- Talking to their boss.
- Playing solitaire.
- Defrosting chicken.
- Having a related discussion in the chat area with another participant or the producer.
- Folding socks (This was listed TWICE!).

While this list seems to contain some daunting competition for you to keep the participants' attention (especially that "folding socks" distracter), there are ways to keep track of your participants.

Remember that some participants will multi-task, no matter how well-designed your program or how important the content. They try to multi-task in the traditional classroom and they glory in the fact that they can get away with doing it in the synchronous classroom. I have found that the key to this problem is to give them an avenue so they can multi-task and use their excess energy, while keeping them in your realm of control. For example, encourage the use of the chat area and don't discourage off-topic conversations. (This is a great place to take advantage of your producer.) Sometimes, you can even "trick" them into thinking they are breaking the rules.

REAL-WORLD EXAMPLE

While I was facilitating a recent workshop for new synchronous trainers, one of my participants said he did not like to use the chat function to communicate with other participants. He felt it was distracting and rude. After all, he couldn't get away with side conversations in a traditional setting.

This comment kicked off a conversation about participant cues. If some participants were having a chat conversation about the event topic, it would indicate that they were interested in the topic and were anxious to share ideas. If the thread was off-topic, they either were not interested in the topic or found the pace too slow. By allowing the chat to occur, the trainer or producer could identify the distractions and find ways to include these participants in the class—either by having them share their on-topic ideas or by trying to engage them in other ways.

I asked what would happen to these distracted participants if we disabled the chat function. After a few minutes of discussion, the group decided these same individuals would probably be answering email or making phone calls while watching the class from the corner of their eye. The trainers would have no way of knowing. If someone is going to multi-task anyway, I'd rather have him or her in the chat area so I can manage the situation.

Reading Participants' Cues

Since synchronous trainers do not have the benefit of eye contact, they miss the traditional visual cues—glazed-over looks of boredom, confused expressions, intent frustration, and so forth. But because eye contact and body language are not available, you'll need to tune in to some different cues—detected by looking for the "invisible energy" coming through bandwidth. These clues are subtle, but can help you manage the class. For example:

- Note how long it takes for the group to provide feedback and answer polls. If it is taking much longer than you expected, they are probably not paying close attention or do not understand the content.

- Use the feedback mechanisms that are built into the classroom. What feedback are you receiving from these tools? For example, the "Yes" and "No" buttons can be a way for participants to nod or shake their heads.

- Look at the quantity of feedback you are receiving. Are the participants raising their hands? Sending chat messages? Asking and answering questions? If not, they may have tuned out.

Also consider how you (the trainer) are feeling. If you feel that the program is dragging, the participants are probably really running out of steam. It's time for a break or an energizer. You never know what the result will be. Take a moment to read about one of my experiences:

REAL-WORLD EXAMPLE

I was teaching a class on a December evening from my home in New England. I noticed a very low energy period, so for a change of pace, I asked the participants to get up and look out the windows nearest their desks and report back on what they saw. Their answers were more eye-opening than I expected:

- A participant in New England said it was a dreary early winter evening—dark with cold rain coming down.
- A participant in Southern California reported a sunny late afternoon, a pleasant 75 degrees. The beach view made it even better.
- A participant in Idaho didn't have a window—and was quite jealous of the others!
- A participant in New Jersey didn't participate in the energizer. Too bad for him.
- A participant in Australia looked out onto a beautiful summer morning—the next day! That participant made all of the rest of us jealous.

This energizer created interest among the participants and re-duced feelings of isolation. Interest in the program was rekindled as well.

The world got smaller in that five-minute period—for all of us.

If your participants are unresponsive or slow to volunteer, you might have to force class participation. For instance, you could have all participants raise their hands before you ask a question, then call on them in the order their hands were raised. You'll have to mix this up occasionally (call on them in reverse order, for example). The less predictable you are, the more your participants will have to stay tuned-in. Conversely, if your participants are talking over each other and interrupting, you might have to take the microphones away and hand them out only as you acknowledge speakers.

Using the Collaboration Tools

Take advantage of the many different communication features of-fered by synchronous classroom applications. For example, conduct a brainstorming activity in the chat area to engage kinesthetic learners who need to do something physical. Group whiteboard ac-tivities appeal to kinesthetic learners as well as visual learners, who like graphic representations of ideas. You can gauge interest and comprehension by participants' level of participation in these exer-cises. Instant collaboration tools can also reduce the isolation that participants feel when they are remote from the trainer.

An important point to remember about these collaboration tools is that they can help save time—a valuable commodity in the synchronous classroom. For example, instead of having all partici-pants in a ten-person class answer a question verbally, have them type their answers in the chat room and give them some time to re-view the answers provided by their peers. You can then respond to comments as appropriate.

▶ By having participants collaborate concurrently (for example, having the entire class work in the chat area or on the whiteboard) everyone is engaged at the same time. If participants have to do something, chances are they won't walk away from their computers.

The Synchronous Whiteboard

The whiteboard is one of the most collaborative tools in the synchronous classroom—especially for visual learners. It allows for instant visual communication over a long distance and invites everyone to participate. Kinesthetic learners also appreciate the ability to interact physically with the tool because it helps to keep their attention focused.

Whiteboards typically contain some combination of the following tools: pencil, eraser, text, color, lines, and various shapes. Each vendor offers different whiteboard features. Some are object-oriented. Some allow you to import files into the whiteboard and use them as you would a prepared flip chart. My favorite feature of the whiteboard tools is the ability for multiple people to write on the whiteboard at one time.

Tips for Facilitating Synchronous Whiteboard Exercises

Here are some tips for successful whiteboard exercises:

- *Plan the exercises*. If you know that you want to have six people write responses on the whiteboard, prepare a grid with six boxes so participants can clearly identify their individual spaces.

- *Encourage creativity*. Instead of instructing participants to "type their responses," encourage them to draw illustrative pictures, use different colors and fonts, and highlight important parts of their drawings.

- *Let it get messy*. Sometimes participants go over their own assigned spaces and accidentally write in someone else's box. So what? If they are concerned about "crossing over" they will tend to be less creative.

- *Involve everyone.* If only a few participants are writing ideas on the whiteboard, ask the rest to comment on the ideas or to interpret the pictures.

- *Play games.* Have participants draw in missing parts of diagrams, complete crossword puzzles, or play quiz games. This is a great way to reinforce content, energize the audience, and have fun.

REAL-WORLD EXAMPLE
Whiteboard Exercise Example #1

Sometimes the tools produce interactions you don't expect. I was working with a client group that wanted to minimize the use of the whiteboard function because, in their traditional programs, they were trying to get away from flip charts and whiteboards that did not add anything to their programs. They saw the synchronous whiteboard tool as serving the same function.

Despite their concerns, I managed to sneak in some whiteboard collaboration exercises that engaged all of the participants in the program—and created a new avenue for learning. Some of the best exercises in the program were conducted using the whiteboard. Obviously, this wasn't the same old flip chart!

What feedback do I hear from this client now? "Let's do some more whiteboard exercises!"

Whiteboard Exercise Example #2

One of the best pre-class exercises I can remember is when I was facilitating a program with a "baseball theme." I asked people to log on between ten and fifteen minutes prior to the official start time so we could troubleshoot any last-minute problems and make sure class began when scheduled. As participants logged on, I asked them to "autograph" the picture of the baseball that we had created on the whiteboard. They were allowed to use nicknames, like "John 'Slugger' Smith." When they were done, they moved to the chat area to discuss how they hoped to "hit a home run" with their current initiative.

While participants were doing this, I helped people with technical problems and reinforced how to use the whiteboard and chat tools. This fun interaction set the tone for a fast-moving and effective program.

The Chat Area

The most common use for the chat area is to address technical support issues and answer content-related questions—especially anonymous questions. While this is an important function, it is a shortsighted view of what can be a very powerful interaction tool.

Chat exercises can be a great outlet for the excess energy typical of kinesthetic learners. The chat area can be used to capture the results of brainstorming exercises. It offers a different communication method to break up lectures. If your chat feature allows you to save the results of a chat interaction, you can post assignments, expectations, and participant feedback and use the results later in the class or after the class.

Sometimes you might want to ask for feedback from all of the participants at the same time without spending too much time on the exercise. Using the chat to accomplish this keeps everyone engaged and minimizes the amount of time it takes to hear from everyone.

Tips for Facilitating Chat Exercises

Here are some tips for successful chat exercises:

- *Provide time boundaries*. I once made the mistake of telling participants to "take a minute to record your thoughts in the chat area." When I stopped the exercise at thirty seconds, I heard complaints from some participants who were expecting the full minute. Give specific time limits for chat exercises, and let people know when they have fifteen seconds left. This will allow those who need more time to budget their time and let those who respond more quickly know that they should get ready to refocus on the class.

- *Spelling doesn't count!* Let participants know that they need not be anxious about spelling and grammar while using the chat feature. The time allotted is for idea development and communication and should not be spent on proofreading.

- *Be specific about the anticipated outcome.* Make sure participants know exactly what you want them to do and how you expect them to report their results. The better your instructions, the more effective the exercise will be.

- *Allow participants to reflect on peer responses.* It is important for participants to have time to compare and contrast their own responses with everyone else's. Encourage this by saying (or typing) things like: "I'd like everyone to take a look at Mary's response—and then take thirty more seconds to record what you think led her to make that decision. Respond using the chat room."

Real-World Example
Chat Exercise Example #1

Using a chat room in a rich synchronous environment can truly allow two separate activities to occur at the same time. For example, one very successful exercise that we use for a warm-up involves the use of both a trainer and a producer.

As participants log in to class, they are presented with a whiteboard grid asking whether they have completed their prework, whether they brought their printed workbook to class, and other administrative questions. The producer verifies that they have all necessary materials and helps them adjust their audio. As participants complete these tasks, they are sent to the chat room to work with the trainer. Here, the trainer debriefs the prework using a predesigned exercise that accommodates people joining the exercise at different times. The producer then works with the next person who logged in. Once the producer has checked in all the participants, he or she can call missing participants or assist participants with more troublesome technical issues. The participants in the chat area do not have to worry about that—they are being kept usefully engaged.

Chat Exercise Example #2

You can use the whiteboard and chat in combination with each other very successfully.

We often use the chat area as a brainstorming tool. For example, using the chat area we might ask participants in an entry-level management training program, "What concerns about managing others keep you up at night? Take two minutes to explain your concern—using specific examples if necessary." (Since this question is planned, we have it typed already in a separate document. We just copy and paste it into the chat area to save time and to minimize spelling errors.)

After the two-minute period, we ask participants to review one another's responses. We then choose one response, copy it out of the chat area, and paste it onto the whiteboard—where the entire group discusses possible ways to address this concern.

The beauty of this exercise is that it allows participants to generate and communicate individual concerns, share them with their peers, and then participate in a collaborative exercise to discover a solution. We can then save the chat interactions as a text file, edit the text file so the postings are anonymous, and share the group concerns with human resources to help plan future programs.

Regardless of your diligent preparation and detailed scripts, synchronous training requires some quick thinking. So be flexible—lots of last-minute, unanticipated problems can occur when working remotely with participants via web technology. It's essential that you keep the learning moving and manage high-stress situations with grace. And be creative; you'll need to be able to do damage control, move forward, and meet the course objectives, regardless of the circumstances. Use your creative insights and adapt your leader guides to your participants' changing needs.

A Note on Class Size

What is the optimum class size? It depends. While virtual classrooms can accommodate literally hundreds of participants at the same time, such large numbers are not appropriate for hands-on interactive training programs.

In my experience, a program should contain no more than 75 percent of the number of participants you would invite to the same program taught in a traditional manner. It is challenging to manage any type of classroom environment. Because of the introduction of new technologies, the geographical dispersion of the audience, and the loss of eye contact and body language, a synchronous environment is even more challenging than a traditional classroom.

> ▶ There are some instances in which a large audience is appropriate. Corporate announcements and auditorium lectures are examples.

Having too many participants is challenging for the trainer. It also increases the likelihood that an individual will become disassociated from the learning experience. If you have complex content that requires all participants to interact with applications and other types of content, you may consider enrolling no more than 50 percent of the number you would allow for a traditional classroom.

Rules of Thumb

The following are some general facilitation tips for synchronous trainers:

- *Learn the technology.* This guideline cannot be overstated. You must be able to manage the technology and transition to new technologies as needed. This takes practice, time, and a commitment to learning virtual classroom applications.

- *Multi-task*. In the synchronous learning world, trainers are always doing several things at once, for example, writing on the whiteboard while discussing content or answering questions in the chat area while managing an exercise. It is important to your success as a facilitator that you are comfortable managing many tasks at one time.

- *Implement and model ground rules*. Ground rules are critical to the success of any synchronous learning experience. As a trainer, you should set the ground rules, model them, and maintain their usage throughout the class. I explain this concept in more detail in Chapter 6, Working with Synchronous Participants.

- *Create interactions and have participants do something every three to five minutes*. This could mean interactions with people, technology, or a participant workbook. It could also mean thinking or writing! It is important to re-engage your participants as often as possible. While much of this is built into the course design, there will be times when you will need to create interactions on the spot. Doing this keeps participants focused on the program and helps to ensure that the audience is still present.

- *Be a team player*. Your success depends on your ability to work with a variety of people during a synchronous learning experience, including assistant trainers, technical support, and geographically dispersed participants. This type of learning is a group effort, and successful facilitators work with all members of "the show"—behind the scenes, during the learning session, and after the event.

- *Plan your program*. Create a detailed facilitation plan that includes planned ad-libs, anecdotes, instructional strategies, technical tips, and other pertinent information. Remember that there is a lot to manage in a virtual classroom, so be prepared for anything.

- *Design with the available tools in mind.* There are many tools available in synchronous classrooms that are not available in traditional classrooms, like chat, web browsers, and application sharing. Learn these tools and use a variety of them. Variety helps to keep your participants engaged.

- *Vary your instructional strategies to maximize engagement.* Chances are that a one-hour lecture will not be successful in a virtual classroom. Instead, incorporate discussions, breakout sessions, brainstorming. . . . The options are endless.

- *Keep it human.* Make sure the design does not take the participants out of the process. Learning is a social activity, and participants need a personal touch. Do not fall into the trap of talking to your computer screen instead of to your participants. Use participants' names, recall things they said earlier, and develop relationships.

- *Plan for technology gaps.* When launching an application or setting up breakout rooms, there is often a gap of up to thirty seconds while the technology is being prepared. This "dead air" is enough to make your less secure participants wonder whether they are experiencing technical difficulties and prompt your less tolerant participants to jump into an unrelated task. Anticipate that gap, and design a meaningful personal or chat activity to fill the time.

- *Have fun and relax!* Remember that you will not have perfect classes every time. If you go with the flow and embrace the experience, your expertise and enthusiasm will relax your participants, create the learning environment, and help you prepare for next time.

- *Plan for a recovery period.* A common error for new synchronous trainers is to plan meetings or other activities immediately following a synchronous event. In a traditional classroom, much of a trainer's energy comes from the participants. We can see, hear, and experience their reactions—and we respond to them. In a synchronous classroom, we cannot directly draw from participants' energy, so we need to create our own energy to make the class dynamic and interactive. This can be exhausting, and trainers often need some downtime to recuperate.

QUESTIONS ABOUT THIS CHAPTER:

IDEAS AND APPLICATIONS:

4

Synchronous Classroom Management

I once heard the synchronous classroom described as "the best and worst combination of traditional classroom training and asynchronous web-based training."

Some of the "worst" aspects of traditional classroom training are the logistics of preparing the classroom, the content, and the participants. The same logistics are associated with the synchronous classroom as well—with some extra technology and learning environment considerations thrown in for good measure.

In this chapter I illustrate some practical considerations for ensuring a smooth and effective event. In Appendix B, I've included a series of classroom management checklists for you to use in planning your events. Keep track of anything you run into that is not captured on this checklist—it will make planning easier the next time!

Managing Time and Scheduling Issues

Sometimes it seems more difficult to gain commitment for short synchronous sessions than for all-day offsite programs. When potential conflicts arise in a participant's schedule, more often than not the synchronous event seems to be less essential.

As a synchronous trainer, you will always be competing with other participant commitments. You won't always win that competition—but there are some things you can do to maximize attendance and maximize your online time.

- *Be sensitive to time differences.* Participants in your class might be logged on from different time zones. Try to avoid scheduling classes that will be very early, very late, or during meal times for a majority of participants. Be very clear about the time zone in your enrollment letter. I suggest you include the start time for every participating time zone, for example: 12 p.m. Eastern, 11 a.m. Central, 10 a.m. Mountain, and 9 a.m. Pacific.

- *Don't coddle latecomers.* When someone logs in ten minutes, thirty minutes, or even one hour late, don't stop your exercise to bring him or her up to the rest of class. You don't have the luxury of an eight-hour day where you can cancel a break or ask people to stay an extra twenty minutes. When I notice someone logging in after the class is in full swing, I generally say something like: "Welcome, Bob. Please meet the producer, Mary, in the chat area and she will tell you where we are. Mary, please debrief Bob." The producer can then provide options for the late participant, including the opportunity to attend another program, observe the rest of this program, or participate when it makes sense. If you have opted to utilize your synchronous platform's Record/Playback feature to record the class, inform the participant that he will be receiving instructions on how to access that recording once the class is over.

- *Plan to end your synchronous class on or before the scheduled end time.* Participants will take advantage of the fact that they are learning from their desks. If you tell them the class will be over at noon, chances are someone's lunch appointment will show up right on time. Since the appointment is right there and you are not, there is a good chance you will lose that participant before you are ready. Additionally, if you make a habit of running late, you may discourage participants from enrolling in future classes.

- *Schedule more time than you think you will need.* Unanticipated technical problems can skew your timing; some of this can be made up during class, but you don't want to rush the learning activities. Also, be sure to leave enough time at the end of the event for participants to fill out a course evaluation.

- *Ask participants to log on fifteen minutes early.* In a traditional setting, if all participants walked in the room at 8:30 a.m. for an 8:30 a.m. class, you probably wouldn't start the class for at least ten or fifteen minutes while everyone got settled in. The same is true for synchronous programs. But don't punish people for arriving early by having them do nothing. Use this extra time to conduct audio checks and warm-up exercises.

- *Check in with participants.* Send an email to participants several hours prior to the scheduled class to remind them of the start time (and the time zone!) and to ask them to confirm their attendance. Include the technical support number in that note. If someone does not confirm attendance, assume that he or she will not be attending.

REAL-WORLD EXAMPLE

Most television productions with live audiences have producers who "warm up" the audience before the "talent" starts the show. This occurs before the scheduled "on air" time. The purpose of this warm-up is to help the audience understand its role in the production, explain the different tools they might be expected to use (microphones, response keypads, and so forth), and to get them excited about being part of the show. When the curtain goes up, everyone is comfortable and knows what he or she is supposed to do.

Synchronous trainers and producers can borrow this effective technique. Have participants log on fifteen minutes ahead of time. Use the producer to ensure that the technology is working, that participants have their class materials, and that they remember how to use the communication tools. Use fun activities to encourage less comfortable participants to relax.

When the "talent" gets on stage and the "curtain goes up," you'll be set for a great program.

Determining the Best Length for a Program

I recommend that synchronous programs be roughly ninety minutes without a break or two hours with a fifteen-minute break. (I plan for these breaks in my design—and launch an animated graphic that counts down the minutes for the length of the break. Once the timer counts down to "0," I immediately start class. Ask your media group to help you create these.) Of course, the more interactive your class is, the longer participants will be able to stay involved. One thing is clear—participants will quickly lose interest in a program as short as thirty minutes if their only contribution to the class is looking at the screen and clicking "Yes" or "No" every once in a while. Like any successful training program, it all comes back to sound instructional design.

You may, of course, have content that takes longer than two hours to present. One strategy for these longer programs is to present a live session in the morning, then provide an asynchronous activity, and regroup in the afternoon. This allows you to complete the course in one day and provide adequate time for participants to manage phone calls and other necessary tasks. Some synchronous programs are designed to be presented over several weeks (for example, every Monday for two hours over six weeks). This takes a longer time commitment, and you will need an asynchronous plan for participants who need to miss one or two sessions.

Communciating with Class Participants

Interaction with your participants extends well beyond the day of the synchronous event. For your class to be a success, you will need to communicate with participants before, during, and after class. Here's what I suggest:

- *Create a contact list with the names and phone numbers of your class participants.* Use this if you need to connect with participants prior to class or to assist participants during class. If participants will be using a phone line to dial in, encourage them to give you a cell phone or alternate number so you can contact them during class. Keep your contact list up-to-date and provide your producer with a copy.

- *Make sure your participants have all necessary materials for class.* These may include workbooks, readings, and exercises. A week before class, I generally send out a program description that contains information such as course URLs, date, time, technical support numbers, and prework requirements.

- *Encourage participants to complete any required prework* (readings, supplementary web modules, planning exercises). Not being prepared for class can make it nearly impossible to participate in skills practices and other in-class exercises. Make sure your participants know that failing to do the prework will impact not only their own learning, but also that of their peers. To ensure it is completed, you can password-protect the synchronous event and only distribute passwords to individuals who have sent you an email message proving they have completed the prework exercises.

- *Have participants complete a "tech check" at least one week prior to the synchronous event.* This will ensure that the software is installed and working properly on the PCs they will use for class. For more information about what is entailed in a tech check, refer to Chapter 5, Managing the Technology.

- *Teach participants how to learn.* As a prerequisite to synchronous events, I require that new participants participate in a Learn How to Learn Online class. This program not only covers "point and click" basics of participating in a synchronous classroom, but also explains ground rules, provides guidelines for minimizing distractions, and gives the consequences of coming to class late and neglecting prework. I recommend a basics course like this for any participants who are not familiar with virtual classroom technology; this way, class members will be on an equal playing field for their first synchronous event. A more detailed description of this program is included in Chapter 6, Working with Synchronous Participants.

- *Provide a technical support number in case problems arise during class.* If you are teaching with a producer, it's a good idea for the technical support number to be the producer's cell phone or alternate telephone line.

- *Offer "virtual office hours" or individual synchronous coaching.* When the event is over, offer time for individuals who need additional tutoring to meet you online. Remember that your participants are less familiar with this learning technology than you are and may need some clarification.

- *Make a recording available.* If you successfully record the class, send a note to class participants letting them know that this asynchronous option is available to them if they want reinforcement. View the recording before you make it public to make sure it is what you expected.

Preparing to Facilitate the Class

Your preparation for a synchronous event extends beyond the virtual classroom. If you are new to synchronous training, you might make a checklist for yourself. See Appendix B for sample preparation checklists.

At Least Two Weeks Before the Class

- Reserve the resources you will need, including your producer, your workstation, and the synchronous classroom server. (Your organization may have purchased only a limited number of "seats." Make sure they are not already being used.)

- Coordinate with your producer to determine who will do what during the synchronous event. Indicate these responsibilities in your leader guide.

- Coordinate with your online training administrator to ensure that your participants are enrolled in the system, that your event is scheduled, and that there is a process for supporting participant software installations.

- Communicate with your participants. Send them instructions for attending class, downloading software, and completing prework.

- Review the course content and make sure you are comfortable with it. If you did not design the course yourself, you might ask questions of the instructional designer.

- Coordinate with the instructional designer to make sure the course content on the server contains all the specific information you will require.

- Prepare any reference materials or additional resources that you might access during class. For example, I create a Microsoft Word® document called "Production Text," which includes definitions and other text to paste onto the whiteboard during class. (See Chapter 5, Managing the Technology, for more on this topic.)

- Have a dress rehearsal. After you have validated your content and written your script, rehearse! Invite enough people to ensure that your exercises are fully tested—and ask them to complete any prerequisites to make the experience as realistic as possible. Work with your voice to make sure you are using effective tone and inflection. Remember that your voice is now your number one communication tool.

- Create a plan to handle minor technical issues that might come up during class. For instance, decide whether you will handle these issues yourself or have a producer to assist you. Determine whether your cellular phone will work from where you will be facilitating the course.

- Create a back-up plan. Let's face it—sometimes the technology just doesn't work, no matter how prepared you are. What will you do if the server goes down? If your computer freezes?

If there is a storm and the power goes out? Prepare a back-up plan and a communication plan for participants. You could conduct a conference call, send out an email, or have a rain date. Whatever your plan, your participants should know it.

- Watch a recorded version of the class you will be teaching, if one is available. This is a great way to understand how the content flows, how participants will react, and how exercises work.

On the Day of Class

- Check your own equipment to make sure everything is working properly.
- Check in with participants to verify attendance and answer last-minute questions.

Forty-Five Minutes Prior to Class

- Hang a "Do Not Disturb" sign on your door.
- Arrange to log on as a participant on another PC so you can see the participant interface as well as your own. (Optional)
- Have a pitcher of water, a drinking glass, and some straws ready to go.
- Clear your teaching area of distractions, including other work and email programs.
- Log on for class at least thirty minutes early.
- Arrange your PC window so you can see the text chat area and the virtual classroom window at the same time if your software supports this.
- As participants arrive, have them do a final audio check and encourage them to use the public chat area. Think of it as a virtual "water cooler," where participants can mill around and get to know each other before the class begins. Since synchronous classes often begin with a chat area warm-up exercise, this helps participants get comfortable sending chat messages.

After the Class

- Watch and publish your recordings and communicate access instructions to interested parties. You may decide to edit the recordings to make them more usable. For example, edit out the breaks and extraneous discussions.

  ▶ Instead of recording a class every time it is delivered, consider creating a "master recording" designed for on-demand viewing. This will contain all the content without any extraneous discussions.

- Follow up with participants who had trouble. You might schedule virtual office hours if several participants seemed to have difficulty.

- Write a self-assessment of the class. Make a list of changes and updates to consider the next time you teach the material. Be sure to include the feedback you received from the producer as well as test and evaluation results. Share these results with the instructional designer.

Using Your Leader Guide Effectively

For some reason, when trainers start teaching synchronously, they often decide not to use a leader guide. If you want your online programs to be as interactive and "high-touch" as they are in the traditional classroom, using leader guides becomes even more important. Written effectively, leader guides capture the choreography of the program, documenting what the trainer, the producer, the participants, and the technology are doing. Since they are often all doing something at the same time (sometimes even multiple things!), you should have a detailed plan that explains the design. If you do not, you may discover that your event is much more lecture-oriented than you wanted and that interaction with participants is limited to "Yes/No" questions and a few polls.

Optimally, you will be teaching your synchronous classes from some sort of guide or syllabus. These can vary from task descriptions and checklists to detailed scripts. What you should use depends largely on your personal preference; some synchronous trainers find highly detailed leader guides too constraining, while others appreciate the security of explicit scripts. Regardless of your preference, this section shares some leader guide strategies that our facilitators have found helpful. It also contains sample guide pages to illustrate the techniques. Chapter 2 also provided guidance on creating leader guides.

Leader Guide Design Strategies

Keep the production tasks separate from the facilitation tasks. Ideally, you want to be able to glance at what the producer is doing without letting these tasks distract you. Our solution is to have the production notes and facilitation notes on facing adjacent pages. In this way, you can reference the production tasks while following your own sequence of facilitation tasks. (See Figure 2.1, a simplified version of a leader guide layout.)

Include time guidelines in your leader guide. These serve as reminders and help you get back on track if you find yourself off schedule. At the front of the guide, I give time approximations for each slide. Then I indicate more prominent milestones with timing icons (a watch face). For instance, after the first major exercise, there might be an icon and the message, "You should have one hour left at this point." When you're teaching, it's much easier to see at a glance how much time you have left rather than how many minutes you just spent on a slide (see Figure 4.1). Since the producer has the same information, he or she can monitor the time and provide feedback to the trainer when an exercise takes longer than expected.

FIGURE 4.1   Timing Milestone in a Synchronous Leader Guide.

Facilitation Tasks		
Transition	**SAY:** Now that we have a complete understanding of these concepts, let's practice.	•In Your Own Words. . . .
🕐 **Time Check.** . . . At this point you should have 50 minutes left. **Allow** participants to take a 10-minute break.		

FIGURE 4.2   Highlighted Script.

Facilitation Tasks
SAY: What did you learn during this online session that surprised you?
CALL on individuals one at a time. Make sure that everyone has the opportunity to participate.
After each participant has had an opportunity to contribute, quickly debrief and summarize the remarks.

Highlight the scripting. Our leader guides are a combination of action steps ("CALL on a participant to answer the question") and trainer script ("SAY: Now let's go over the ground rules"). Because of the amount of extra information that might be included, we find it helpful to distinguish the scripted lines with highlighting so the trainer can easily identify the script. (See Figure 4.2.)

Include screenshots of each slide in your leader guide. While you are teaching you should be looking at the classroom interface so you can see the interaction of the participants, but having the screenshots in the guide is very helpful because it allows you to prep while not online. (See Figure 4.2.)

Keep notes and tips separate from the action steps. The notes should serve as reminders without cluttering the instruction. We use a two-column page design that has instructions on the left and notes on the right. (See Figure 4.3.)

FIGURE 4.3 Notes Separated from Action Steps.

Production Tasks		
Setting Up for Class: Production Notes		
Support Tasks	SAY: If you can hear me, please click the "Yes "button. PROVIDE: a microphone to each learner as he or she joins the class and ask him/her to say "Hello."	▷As each learner arrives, verify that he or she can hear you.
	WRITE: the technical support phone number on the current slide. SAY: You should write down the technical support number on a piece of paper in case your computer gives you problems.	▷You should write the technical support number in the public chat area as well.

QUESTIONS ABOUT THIS CHAPTER:

IDEAS AND APPLICATIONS:

5

Managing the Technology

When it comes to working in synchronous classrooms, Murphy's Law applies. What can go wrong will go wrong—eventually. The best approach is to expect the worst and prepare for it. Learning the technology and learning how to anticipate and troubleshoot problems is the best way to ensure your grace under fire.

Creating a Seamless Production

During the synchronous event, you might find yourself using your microphone, writing on the whiteboard, reading a chat message, reviewing survey responses, and referring to your leader guide—all at roughly the same time! It can certainly seem overwhelming, but managing the technology can make your inevitable multi-tasking much easier.

The first thing you will need to do is learn how to use the synchronous classroom technology. Since you can't anticipate everything that will happen during a live event, you will need to know how to manage all the tools and how to troubleshoot as many technical problems as possible.

Your software vendor probably offers a variety of excellent training options in an online format. Take advantage of as many courses as you can, and check out whether recordings are available. Before you can master the "art" of teaching synchronously, you have to master the "science" of the technology. Vendor training is a great start for that.

After you have explored all the facets of the technology, the next step is to practice. Practice on your own, run rehearsals, watch your recordings, and practice again. The more you rehearse, the more comfortable you will feel during live events.

Arranging Your PC Window

Here are some suggestions for organizing your onscreen space:

- To maximize your onscreen real estate, set your screen resolution to 1024 by 768. You'll find this setting in your PC control panel, under the "Display" option (see Figure 5.1). This screen resolution allows you to have the text chat open without blocking the classroom screen.

- Adjust the proportions of both the classroom window and the chat dialog box so that you can see as much of the chat box as possible without blocking the main classroom window. (See Figure 5.2.)

- Open any other files and applications that you might need to reference or share during class. Minimize these screens until you need to reference them.

- Close any applications that you will not need during class. These take up extra system resources that could impact computer performance during the event.

- Reset any special fonts, points, and backgrounds to your default settings. Remember that your own computer settings might be broadcast to your class during application sharing and synchronized web browsing exercises. If you share an application and it does not look like the participant's own version, they may become confused.

FIGURE 5.1   Windows Display Properties: Screen Resolution Settings.

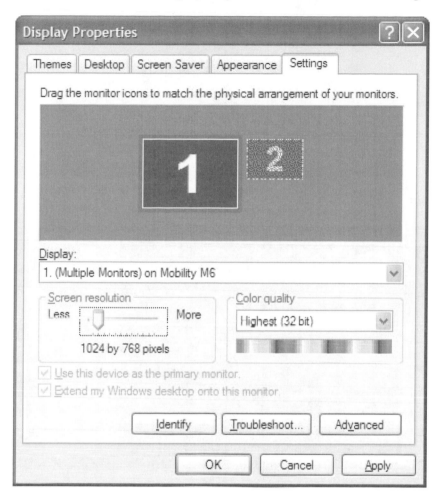

ADVANCED TIP

Ask your technical support person if your trainer workstation supports two monitors. If it does, take advantage of that fact and use a second monitor. It can really simplify and streamline the training process. I like to place my chat window and other necessary applications on the second monitor. This way I can maximize the synchronous classroom and navigate between windows without losing visual contact with my participants.

FIGURE 5.2   Virtual Classroom Window and Chat Area.

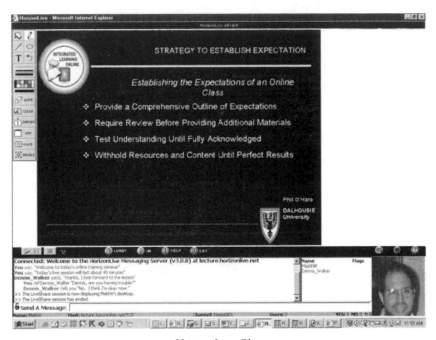

HorizonLive Class

Sharpening Your "Production" Skills

Working with a producer can greatly ease your burden from a technical standpoint. The producer typically handles the technicalities so you can focus more attention on the material and the participants. Even with a producer, you'll need to make sure your own "production" skills are sharp. This section and the next offer some tips for enhancing your (and your producer's) technical savvy and efficiency in the synchronous classroom.

- Use keystrokes and shortcuts. You should be adept at using keystrokes and other shortcuts in the synchronous classroom, especially during chat, whiteboard, and application-sharing exercises. With many synchronous classroom applications, you can use the same keystrokes you're familiar with from the Windows word-processing environment. (You should test them first to make sure they work.) Table 5.1 contains a list of the shortcuts I find most useful.

- Be careful when using the <Ctrl> + keystrokes if participants are talking (such as <Ctrl> + V to paste text). In many synchronous applications, this takes the microphone away from the current speaker.

TABLE 5.1   Keystrokes.

Keystroke	Action	Useful in...
CTRL + c	Copy	Chat area and Whiteboard
CTRL + x	Cut	Chat area and Whiteboard
CTRL + v	Paste	Chat area and Whiteboard
CTRL + z	Undo	Application sharing
CTRL + PgDn	Go to top of next page	Application sharing
CTRL + PgUp	Go to top of previous page	Application sharing
CTRL + End	Go to end of document	Application sharing
CTRL + Home	Go to beginning of document	Application sharing

- If you are using breakout rooms (or a similar feature) for practice and small group exercises, don't set up the breakout rooms too early. In some applications, participants can "step out" of class. If they do, they will need to be reassigned to their breakout rooms. Ideally, the best time to set up breakout rooms is during a break in the class just before the breakout-room exercise.

- Don't type long blocks of text during the synchronous event. If your exercises call for you to place text on the whiteboard or in the chat area, plan to have this text pre-typed in a text document. Keep this document open to copy and paste blocks of material directly from the document to the whiteboard or chat area. This technique saves time and reduces the chance of typing errors. I prepare this document in the course-design phase and save it as "Production Text." Ideally, you'll be working with a course producer who can select and paste the appropriate blocks of text from this document for you; if not, here's another chance for you to multitask!

REAL-WORLD EXAMPLE

One exercise we use frequently deals with asking participants to "think about someone you know who exhibits competence around the skill of [any skill goes here]." We ask them to comment on that person in the public chat area. We know that there are some questions we will want to ask as follow-up to their responses, so we have those typed ahead of time in another application and are ready to copy and paste those questions into the chat area. Here is a typical exercise that would be conducted entirely in the chat area:

PASTE: Everyone: Think of someone at work who is good at [any skill]. What does this person do when he or she is doing this well? Take about ninety seconds to answer this question in the chat area.

When everyone has answered, follow up with these questions using the same format:

PASTE: What exactly does he or she do?

PASTE: What about what he/she does makes him/her effective?

PASTE: Could other people do the same thing?

When everyone has finished, you can ask participants to review their peers' responses and comment on them. If you keep this exercise moving quickly, you give everyone in the class a chance to reflect on and respond to the same questions. You probably would not have the time to conduct this same exercise with everyone verbally.

- Re-purpose participant text chat. By pasting material from the chat area to the whiteboard, you can elaborate on ideas and use them as a springboard for further discussion.

Making the Most of the Medium

Be aware of bandwidth during application-sharing exercises. The typical way to have participants do individual application exercises is to send them into individual breakout rooms to work. This may not be successful if the software application you are trying to share is extremely large or if bandwidth is limited. One way to eliminate this problem is to ask participants to complete the individual work from their desktops instead of from the synchronous classroom. Ask them to keep the classroom open in the background. While they are working, monitor the synchronous classroom and the chat area in case they toggle back to ask questions. Use the chat area to communicate during individual coaching sessions so you do not disturb the other participants, and use the voice option when you want to broadcast to everyone at the same time. Remember, as long as your participants are logged on and using their headsets, they can hear you even if the synchronous classroom is not the active window.

Some software vendors recommend that you avoid talking or giving instructions when changing slides, especially when using a dial-up connection. Your voice may get cut off. This is something you definitely want to test during your dress rehearsal.

Use the "Press to Talk" button only during application sharing and web browsing—not during regular class discussion. This feature tends to encourage trainers to lecture rather than engage participants— and trainers often forget to disengage it when they have finished speaking.

If you are using an animated countdown timer to manage your break periods, take away the participants' whiteboard control. Writing on the screen while the timer is running or changing slides can reset the timer.

Tell participants what to do if you lose your connection. If you drop out of class unexpectedly (and trust me—this happens more than you would like), it can be very confusing for participants. If you are using a producer, arrange for that person to have some quick exercises in his or her "hip pocket" to use as a contingency plan. If you are training without that support, let participants know that if you drop out, they should give you up to five minutes to rejoin the class. If you do not return, one participant should call the designated technical support number for instructions and communicate these to the rest of the class.

If you are doing an application sharing exercise, be aware that some software cannot handle 16-bit applications and test your applications prior to the synchronous event. On the other hand, application sharing can sometimes be a better alternative than synchronous web browsing. If the site requires all participants to log in and/or use passwords, this can take a lot of valuable class time. In this case, application sharing is a better alternative, since only the trainer needs to log in.

Don't panic when things don't go as planned. You will be faced with many surprises—not all of them bad. Take these surprises in stride and strive to minimize their impact on the participants' experiences.

Troubleshooting Technology

Both the trainer and the producer must be able to handle technical issues as quickly and efficiently as possible. When a participant cannot participate due to a technical problem, it is natural to try to analyze and diagnose the problem. Don't do this—it only wastes time! Rather, concentrate on getting the participant up and running and back in the class again.

The "Tech Check"

Perhaps the most important step you can take to avoid technology headaches is to conduct a Tech Check with every participant prior to the day of class. You don't need to check out participants before every synchronous session they attend, but do encourage them to sign up for new checks if they are using a different computer or it has been over six months since they last participated.

A Tech Check answers the following questions for the participant:

- Has the software been installed correctly?
- Does the computer meet the minimum hardware and software requirements suggested by the software vendor?
- Can the participant attain adequate bandwidth to ensure good performance?
- Are there any firewall or access issues that must be resolved?
- Does application sharing work? (*Note:* I have encountered situations where everything but the application sharing was able to get through the firewall.)
- Are the speakers and microphone working and adjusted for best quality?
- Are all software applications required for individual work installed on the machine? Are all versions up-to-date?
- Are all plug-ins required for your program installed and up-to-date? (*Note:* if people have participated in synchronous

sessions before, they need not go through a Tech Check for this. Just send them a link to web content requiring the same plug-in to test the installation.)

Here are some suggestions for conducting the Tech Check:

- Participants should complete the Tech Check at least one week prior to their first scheduled event. If something is not working, they will need time to get it fixed or make other arrangements.
- Be sure participants test using the same equipment they will use for the synchronous event.
- Track Tech Check attendance using your Learning Management System. Make sure that successful completion of this event is a prerequisite for attending any other synchronous classes.
- If possible, have participants test in the same location they will use for the synchronous event. Sometimes participants will test their laptops at home and find they work using dial-up connections. They then decide to participate from work in order to take advantage of the high-speed network, only to discover that they have a firewall or proxy server that prevents them from participating.
- Test under combat conditions. Rehearse with the same number of people you actually expect in class and at the same time of day you expect the class to occur. If your participants will be on dial-up connections, your rehearsal group should be as well. Use the designated trainer workstation and the network from which you plan to teach. Some high-bandwidth exercises such as application sharing and other large programs work fine one-on-one, but slow down the pace considerably when eight or ten people are involved or when the Internet is really busy at certain times of day.

REAL-WORLD EXAMPLE

I find that you lose your bandwidth when you least expect it. I remember once conducting a rehearsal at 5:30 p.m. in the San Jose area. None of the rehearsal participants could maintain their connections to the server. When we contacted the network administrator, he informed us that our experience was typical of network performance in that area at that time of day. His advice: Conduct classes earlier in the day.

Another time I set our trainer and producer up at a client site on the day they were supposed to teach two programs. We had not rehearsed at that site. We assumed that since the client was a well-known, e-commerce provider with a huge investment in network infrastructure, we would have excellent network performance. We were wrong—the trainer and producer were disconnected and reconnected to the class every five minutes or so, and it was incredibly disruptive. We later ascertained that the network was designed to facilitate e-commerce transactions and that those transactions took precedence over all other activity. This was not noticeable to most people, but it was very obvious in the synchronous classroom environment. We had broken our own rule: Test in the same environment in which you are going to teach.

Up and Running and Ready to Participate

Getting participants up and running and ready to participate should be your only goal when troubleshooting during a live event. Don't spend time debating various possibilities—just try to get everything working. When a producer is used, the trainer isn't involved with this process, but still someone has got to make things work. Use the fifteen-minute pre-class warm-up to take care of any last-minute issues.

- Verify that the participant has completed a Tech Check. If not, ask him or her not to participate in that live session.

- If a participant is having trouble logging on to the virtual classroom, verify the logon ID and password and verify that he or she is actually enrolled in the class.

- If a participant cannot launch the synchronous classroom, verify that he or she is using the same computer that was checked out during the Tech Check.

REAL-WORLD EXAMPLE

I remember one particularly high-maintenance participant. He had quite a bit of trouble installing software on his desktop machine. Then he had trouble selecting and setting up his headset. It took about five conversations to get his system running and all of his questions answered.

It turned out that, on the afternoon of the class, he decided he wanted to go home to participate. Five minutes before class was due to start, he called me asking why he could not log in. The reason was simple—he was on a different computer than we had set up and there was no software installed!

- If a participant's audio is not working, verify that the microphone and speakers are plugged in properly. Plugging things into the wrong outlets is the most common technical problem I have encountered.

- If the microphone and headset are plugged in correctly, try having the participant rerun the audio test that is provided by the synchronous classroom software package.

- If problems persist, ask the participant to close the synchronous classroom and browser and log on again.

- Have the participant reset the Internet connection if he or she is using a dial-up connection.

- If all else fails, have the participant reboot the computer and start over.

  ▶ You should include these steps in the participant workbook. Many participants can get themselves up and running with minimal disruption to the class.

- If nothing works, provide a technical support contact that is not involved in the current session and follow up with that participant after class to reschedule or to provide a recording.

- Don't hold up a whole class indefinitely to deal with one person's technical difficulties. You have a very short period with your participants, and they will quickly lose interest if your attention is not focused. Use a producer to assist with technical problems, or ask the struggling participant to attend a different session.

- If the participant's audio is functioning but with long delays, have him or her close all other open applications (except for the Internet browser and the virtual classroom window).

- Sometimes major Internet events can really slow things down. We can't do much about this; if heavy Internet traffic causes major delays, consider rescheduling your synchronous event. Be aware of what's happening, and don't be afraid to have a "Plan B."

REAL-WORLD EXAMPLE

I was teaching a class to dial-up participants on the day that Kenneth Starr, the independent counsel investigating scandals associated with the Clinton presidency, published his extensive report on the Internet. I did not download that report—but at the time, it seemed as though everyone else in the world did. The results: All of the participants' connections slowed down to the point where we could not move forward with class.

Troubleshooting Rules of Thumb

- While some people have great results using a 28.8 kpbs connection, these results are not consistent. I always request that participants have a 56 kpbs modem and at least a 40 kpbs connection.

- If you or your participants are using non-standard audio input or output devices (for example, a wireless microphone) you may need to change your Windows audio defaults. When I use a wireless or a stand-alone studio microphone, I need to select "Line Balance" instead of "Mic Balance" in the Windows Recording control panel. Every time I launch the virtual classroom, I need to adjust this setting. Make sure you test your audio device and make note of what you need to adjust in order to maximize performance.

- If you would like to use any bandwidth-intensive media, like Quicktime® movies or Flash® animation, have your participants download this content ahead of time and access it from their hard drives. Your software platform might facilitate this process. If it does not, ask participants to view the media ahead of time, or have it ready to go when they log on to the class so they can toggle to it at the appropriate time.

- If, after a chat or application-sharing exercise, you or a participant tries to speak but cannot activate the microphone, it is probably because the chat or application is the active window— not the synchronous classroom. Just click the synchronous classroom window and try again.

QUESTIONS ABOUT THIS CHAPTER:

IDEAS AND APPLICATIONS:

6

Working with Synchronous Participants

Sometimes I think to myself, "If it were not for the participants always asking questions and taking up my time, my life would be a lot easier." Of course, most of the time I remember that serving the needs of the participants is my ultimate goal. This guide would not be complete without considering this group.

Synchronous training cannot occur without participants. Although participants have a wide range of backgrounds, skills, and technical experience, all must learn to navigate the synchronous learning environment. We must be aware that participants need to "learn how to learn" all over again in this new medium.

In order to train successfully in the synchronous environment, you must be a synchronous participant first! Take as many classes as you can and concentrate on how you feel and how you learn. After you've walked a mile in the shoes of a participant, you'll be much better prepared to take on the role of synchronous trainer.

The Participant Experience

Since kindergarten, or even earlier, we have been learning in pretty much the same way. We go to the trainer's location, we watch and listen to the trainer, and when we leave, we have learned something. (In theory, anyway.) We send signals to the trainer by nodding our heads, raising our hands, yawning, and changing our faces to express understanding, confusion, doubt, and a myriad of other emotions.

We know how this works, and we understand our role in the process.

Now picture a new synchronous participant—let's say it is you.

After more than twenty years of learning in the traditional manner, you are entering the world of synchronous learning. Let's assume you are willing and able to give this environment a chance.

Here is what you have to contend with:

- You don't need to travel to sunny Atlanta (or Akron). You get to stay at your desk and learn from there. And if you are in your office, you will be available to take care of any little emergencies as they come up.

- Your live, "face-to-face" time will be short—maybe one or two ninety-minute sessions. Much of the information that would have been given to you in lecture format is now your responsibility to learn asynchronously. So you need to make sure you read the book, take the tutorial, or watch the video.

- You have to stare at a computer screen for two hours at a stretch—and hope you can find new ways of sending messages now that you have lost eye contact and body language. You do not have other participants in proximity with whom to share or commiserate before class, during breaks, and when the trainer's back is turned.

So do you have a chance? Will you learn anything? Will those around you take the fact that you are in training seriously?

Your experience will have much to do with the tools and training you were given prior to the event. In essence, you need to learn how to learn all over again.

Learning How to Learn Online

In many organizations, the first ten to fifteen minutes of a program are spent teaching first-time synchronous participants the "point and click" of the synchronous class. This amount of time is generally ample for learning the basics of communication and navigation, but it is not enough to master learning in this environment. It is also very tedious for participants who have attended synchronous events in the past.

I suggest that you create you own version of a "Learn How to Learn Online" program and set it up in your learning management system as a prerequisite to attending a content-related class. Offer it regularly. Everyone should be required to attend—even those who are technically oriented. As I said, this is meant to be more than a point-and-click tutorial. During the program, give participants permission to be frustrated and ask them to share their frustrations during the program. You want to alleviate those frustrations now and not let them carry over to content-oriented programs.

A typical sixty-minute (seventy-five with a warm-up) agenda for a learning to learn program looks like this:

- *Warm-up*. This takes place fifteen minutes prior to class start. As participants log on, you conduct a last-minute trouble-shooting session and teach whiteboard and chat tools using fun exercises. This gives participants a chance to experiment in a low-risk environment. I find that, during their first twenty minutes in the synchronous classroom, participants are not listening to the trainer anyway—they want to play. Give them the chance to do it.
- *Introductions*. Introduce the training team using photographs— and explain their qualifications to teach the course. Then let the participants introduce themselves in a creative way— using the chat area, whiteboard, voice, or a combination.
- *Tools overview*. Train the participants how to use all of the communication tools in detail. Use accelerated learning techniques (games, word associations, varied instructional techniques) to make participants as comfortable as possible using the tools.
- *Ground rules*. This is a new learning environment, so there are new ground rules to facilitate the process. Introduce and rein-

force them now so that future classes will be better for everyone. (A sample set of ground rules is located later in this chapter.)

- *The learning environment.* Give the participants some guidance on how to set up their learning environment to maximize learning and minimize disruptions. This is a good time to explain your organization's policy about being able to learn at your desk without interruption. (Some guidelines around the learning environment are provided later in this chapter.)

- *Program details.* This is critical information; this is the time for you to explain your policy on prework, participation, and the different technologies supporting the course. Take this opportunity to explain the e-learning initiative in your organization and how synchronous training fits in.

REAL-WORLD EXAMPLE

I recently conducted several programs, including a Learn How to Learn Online session, for a client. One participant would not participate in the Learn How to Learn Online session because he had attended synchronous sessions at his previous organization. When he got to class, he figured out the technology pretty quickly, but he was very surprised that I called on him when he did not volunteer. He had left his email and instant messenger on and was surprised at the need to interact. He also neglected to complete his prework exercises, not realizing that we would not review the content in depth during the synchronous class. He came in expecting a passive learning experience and found something quite different.

Ground Rules

Here is a list of typical ground rules used in classes. You can run an exercise around this that calls on participants to explain why each point is important. Then build on their responses. This will take a little time to go through, so keep the pace moving. (Please note that these ground rules are written as if a participant were reading them.)

- *Turn off email and phones and clear other distractions away from your training area.* This is important because it is easy to answer the phone or pick up some work and lose track of what is going on in the class. The trainer will not know that you have "checked out" so he or she won't be able to re-engage you successfully.

- *Participate and prepare to be called on by name.* This is important because the synchronous environment lends itself to interaction. Participation will keep you engaged and move the class along. If participation is low, the trainer needs to be able to call on people without physical cues.

- *Raise your hand if you have an immediate question or comment.* When you click the "raise hand" button on your screen, an indicator appears next to your name. This is important because the trainer cannot tell by looking at you if you are confused on a particular point or have something to add.

- *Be patient waiting for a response to your chat messages.* This is important because the trainer cannot do everything at once. Be patient and trust that you will receive a response to your notes.

- *If you leave the program, please send a chat to the trainer when you leave and when you return.* This is important because the trainer must know whether he or she can call on you—and that you are not having technical difficulties.

The Effective Learning Environment

Ideally, participants should be in private rooms while participating in a synchronous environment. In reality, most participants will learn from their desks. To learn effectively from their desks, participants must:

- Tell co-workers they will be in a class.
- Post a sign indicating when class will be over.
- Use a headset instead of speakers to minimize workplace disruptions.
- Ignore people around them who are signaling for attention.
- Turn off the telephone ringer.
- Turn off pagers and cell phones.
- Turn off email and instant message alerts.
- Remove all other tasks and distractions from their desks.

> ▶ Using a telephone conference call poses some special challenges. Ask participants to mute their phones when not speaking so extraneous sounds are not picked up. Also, tell participants not to put their phones on hold. If a person's telephone system has a "music on hold" feature, it can be very annoying and puts the event on hold until that person returns. Participants should cancel any call-waiting features (often this is accomplished by dialing 70* before dialing the conference call number) so the call is not interrupted. Finally, make sure participants know they need to raise their hands before asking questions and not jump in and interrupt.

REAL-WORLD EXAMPLE

One trainer mailed a length of "Police Line—Do Not Cross" tape to all participants for use during a synchronous class. A participant placed this tape across his office door during the program—and it worked so well that he continued to use it during other periods when he did not want to be disturbed!

Participant Guides

Often forgotten in synchronous design, a well-designed participant guide can often be a critical success factor in a synchronous program.

When you use a participant guide, take pains to ensure that the guide is not simply a book containing copies of the screens used in the program. You want to be able to direct the participants' focus, and having all the screens printed out on paper can encourage the participants' eyes to be on the paper instead of on the screen.

Instead of replicating the screens, the participant guide should complement them and help to support class interactions. For example, instead of lecturing for five minutes around three bullet points on a screen, ask the participants to read about them in a participant guide article and then answer questions located at the end of the article in the chat area. Debrief their answers verbally, and move on to the next interaction.

See Figure 6.1 for a sample participant guide table of contents.

FIGURE 6.1   Sample Participant Guide Table of Contents.

SYNCHRONOUS PARTICIPANT GUIDE

Table of Contents

Course Description and Contact Information

Technical Set-Up and Requirements

Technical Support Information

Creating an Effective Online Learning Environment

Disaster Recovery Techniques

Synchronous Participation Ground Rules

Prework Assignment

  What if I don't do the prework?

Reading

Course Exercises

Breakout Room Instructions

Take-Home Assignment

To Print or Not to Print?

In order to avoid participants toggling from the participant guide to the synchronous classroom during a live event, it is essential that they all have printed copies before class begins.

We have found that some audiences, especially those that spend most of their time traveling, are challenged by the need to print anything out from email themselves. If you are working with a "printer-challenged" group, you will need to mail the guide to everyone at least two weeks prior to the class.

If you do decide to email the participant guide, I strongly suggest converting your document to "PDF" format before sending it. This ensures that all participants will have the same page numbering, no matter what their printer type or settings. It can lead to confusion and cause a severe disruption if you are directing participants to incorrect pages during the live program.

If you are sending PowerPoint® slides, make sure that you include page numbering on your slides so you can reference them appropriately during class. Participants may decide to print more than one slide per page. Again, that can cause confusion during a live class.

Participant Guide Content

The participant guide should contain a variety of materials, some specific to the program and some "boiler plate" information that should be generically included.

Suggested participant guide contents include:

- *Program-specific information.* Include access information, class date(s) and time(s), attendance policy, and trainer information. This will need to be customized for every class and is well-suited for a cover letter. Be very clear about time zone information.
- *Prework information.* Include access information, due dates, specific instructions, and the result of not completing the

prework. For example, if participants do not complete a test prior to the class, they will not receive the password to enter the class. Also, if participants need to capture any information that they need to bring to class, make sure that there is room to write that information. (Remember that participants often neglect to complete prework for traditional classes. Use this opportunity to reinforce how critical pre-event preparation is to the synchronous learning format.)

- *Content-specific information.* Include articles, screen shots, breakout room instructions, and any exercises that can be made more effective by providing supplemental instructions. Also include places for participants to take notes.

REAL-WORLD EXAMPLE

We have found that participants have a more difficult time understanding directions in a synchronous classroom, so it helps dramatically if you incorporate directions to all independent and small group exercises in the participant guide. Before you have them start an exercise, explain the directions and direct them to the appropriate page in the participant guide. Also remind them that you will be monitoring the private chat area so they can ask additional questions.

- *Software information.* Include vendor quick reference cards, downloading instructions, troubleshooting tips, and technical support information.
- *"Learn How to Learn Online" information.* Include how to enroll for the prerequisite class, ground rules, and learning environment tips.

Managing Participant Challenges

You might also include some guidance on managing and communicating personal issues. For example, I have found that dyslexic participants sometimes have problems using chat or reading the whiteboard and that colorblind people have trouble reading the whiteboard or content slides. A participant for whom English is a second language may also have some specific concerns. In a traditional classroom, trainers can often support these participants by interpreting and responding to body language. Obviously, that cannot occur in a synchronous environment. If trainers know about these challenges ahead of time, it can alleviate some distress and confusion during the live event.

In the front of the participant guide (or in an introductory email note to participants) encourage participants to let you know if they are dealing with any learning challenges that might be amplified by computer-delivered learning. Assure them that their information will be kept confidential. Ask them whether they have any suggestions for you (the trainer) that can help them learn. Keep track of these suggestions for when you encounter similar challenges.

QUESTIONS ABOUT THIS CHAPTER:

IDEAS AND APPLICATIONS:

7

Synchronous Events

This chapter provides some direction on what should be considered when producing synchronous programs. It is focused on different types of events such as eMeetings, expert presentations, webinars, and training events.

You can produce several types of events using synchronous technology. Some can be pulled together in a minimal amount of time using few resources. Some take quite a bit of time and many more resources to organize. (See Figure 7.1.)

eMeetings

When the goal of your event is to allow a geographically dispersed work group to collaborate or share information, an eMeeting can be very successful. These events are usually about an hour long and can be put together relatively quickly. Many synchronous classroom platforms have special eMeeting versions that are especially designed to accommodate this type of event.

Agendas for the eMeeting should be sent out with the meeting invitation, and some basic slides should be prepared. The person who initiated the meeting could moderate it, or a producer could be used to manage the technology if no one on the team feels comfortable with it.

FIGURE 7.1.   Synchronous Event Continuum.

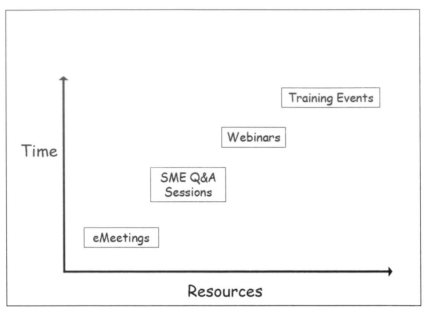

eMeetings are a great way to bring people together and keep everyone in the meeting involved. While many conferences calls are passive experiences where one person reports and everyone else listens, the addition of synchronized visuals and collaborative tools can make meetings more productive and worthwhile.

Expert Q&A

One of the advantages of a synchronous classroom over a traditional classroom is that it is relatively easy to involve a subject-matter expert (SME) in an event. Instead of spending time traveling to and from classes, SMEs can continue to work and log into classes with minimal interruption to their schedules. Participants appreciate having immediate access to expertise, and experts have the opportunity to evangelize their messages.

A word of caution: Organizations see these benefits and ask experts to utilize the technology to teach "classes" on their subjects. This can cause some problems. Many experts have no experience in design or facilitation, and therefore they create text-heavy slides and deliver lengthy lectures. Because they may not have a lot of experience with the technology, and these programs may have fast turnaround requirements, the available collaboration tools often go unused.

To make these programs more effective, consider using a "Talk Show" approach. Use an experienced synchronous producer to manage the technology and moderate the session. Several weeks ahead of time (or as far ahead as scheduling allows) the producer and expert should meet to plan how the content could best be presented. A good rule of thumb is that the expert should plan on preparing content that fills 50 percent of the scheduled event time. For example, a sixty-minute event should contain thirty minutes (or so) of lecture and thirty minutes for questions, discussions, and collaboration.

If you have multiple experts involved in the event, the producer should find out what types of questions each expects to be answering so he or she can direct chat comments to the appropriate person. The producer can also control timing and moderate open discussions. Let the experts focus on the topics of their expertise.

Make sure you don't call these "training" programs. This implies that participants will be able to "do" something after the event is complete. Rather, call them "expert sessions" or "overviews." Sending out materials ahead of time will help some participants formulate questions. Also, prepare some typical questions ahead of time. The producer can ask these questions to jump-start conversations with participants. Keep these sessions to about an hour.

Webinars

Webinars are, essentially, highly produced expert sessions. Use webinars when making important announcements or conducting marketing campaigns. The audience can generally be large (thirty or more participants) and may contain clients, prospects, vendors, or even stockholders.

Start planning these events at least one month ahead of time and use an instructional designer to create the program. Because of the high profile of these events, they should be very tightly designed. The audience should be invited far enough ahead of time to allow them to download any software and test the synchronous environment on their own computers. You may decide that, in order to minimize technical issues, a conference call is a better choice than Internet audio. Multiple rehearsals are critical. Record the rehearsals if you can, so you can critique your performance and fix any problems.

Besides the experts and producer, have a technical support person available online during the event to help with any issues that may come up. Keep these sessions to about an hour.

Learning Events

Most of this guide has been written to prepare you to produce a learning event. If you want participants to be able to do something new, you are designing a learning event. These are characterized by collaborative interactions among participants, some type of assessment, and potentially work that is to be completed before and after the live event. Make sure that you can test your learning objectives in the environment. For example, if an objective requires that you observe a computer engineer install a router, you may not be able to achieve that objective in the synchronous classroom. You may need to hold off on that until you can observe the engineer in some kind of lab condition.

A Final Thought

In *The Synchronous Trainer's Survival Guide* I have attempted to capture the lessons I have learned during my tenure as a synchronous trainer. It is truly a survival guide in that, without learning all of these lessons when I did, I would not have "survived" later classes.

I am certain that tomorrow I will learn more lessons that I will want to share, just as I am certain that many of you have ideas that could add value and insight to future editions of this guide. I look forward to hearing your ideas and learning from you.

I'll "see" you online!

QUESTIONS ABOUT THIS CHAPTER:

IDEAS AND APPLICATIONS:

Appendices

These additional resources to assist you with your synchronous initiative are on the following pages. I hope you find them to be useful.

- Synchronous Software Features Checklist
- Synchronous Classroom Management Checklists
- Recommended Resources for Synchronous and Blended e-Learning
- A Glossary of Terms

Synchronous Software Features Checklist

Use this checklist to document the specifics of your particular synchronous training platform. Bring it to synchronous software training and ask your trainer, or spend the time to investigate on your own.

Software Platform: _____

Version: _____

AUDIO CONSIDERATIONS	NOTES
• What type of audio (full-duplex, half-duplex, telephone conferencing) is available? • Does the software have some kind of "wizard" to test audio settings?	

CHAT CONSIDERATIONS	NOTES
• Is full group chat available? • Is private messaging to the trainer/assistant trainer available? • Is private messaging between participants allowed? • Can a transcript of chat conversations be saved? • Does the transcript include private messaging?	

BREAKOUT ROOM CONSIDERATIONS   NOTES

- What features (application sharing,
  and so forth) are available in the breakout rooms?
- Can participants be pre-assigned to a
  particular room?
- Can participants be moved from room
  to room during an activity?
- Can materials (whiteboards and so on)
  created in breakout rooms be shared
  when the large group is reconvened?

WHITEBOARD CONSIDERATIONS   NOTES

- Can you save whiteboards created during the event?
- Can graphics be pasted or imported to
  the whiteboard?
- How many people can write on the
  whiteboard at once?
- If you return to a slide that you have
  written on, will the comments still be
  there?
- What tools are available for whiteboard
  drawing?
- Can drawing and graphics be moved
  once they are on the whiteboard?

SURVEYS/POLLS/FEEDBACK/   NOTES
  HAND RAISING/PACING/
  COMPREHENSION CONSIDERATIONS

- What survey and/or polling tools are
  available with the platform?
- Can the results be shared with the class?
- Can questions be created spontaneously?
- Is the feedback anonymous/confidential?

TESTING AND EVALUATION   NOTES
  CONSIDERATIONS

- How are evaluation and testing results
  reported?
- How are results saved?

LIVE VIDEO CONSIDERATIONS   NOTES

- What are the hardware and software
  requirements for live video?

DISCUSSION BOARD   NOTES
   CONSIDERATIONS

- Are discussion boards available during
  class?

APPLICATION SHARING   NOTES
   CONSIDERATIONS

- What types of applications can be
  shared?
- What are the bandwidth requirements
  for application sharing?
- Can participants interact with the
  application or just view it?

SYNCHRONIZED WEB BROWSING   NOTES
   CONSIDERATIONS

- Can a participant bring the class to a
  website?
- Can bookmarks be created prior to
  class to speed navigation?
- Does this feature require a specific
  browser?
- Are hyperlinks available to individual
  participants?

RECORD/PLAYBACK   NOTES
   CONSIDERATIONS

- Is special software required to view the
  recordings?
- Can recordings be viewed while not
  connected to the Internet?
- Can trainers stop the recorder and start
  it up again in the same session?

ASSISTANT TRAINER   NOTES
  CONSIDERATIONS

- What can a lead trainer do that an
  assistant trainer cannot do (for example, create breakout rooms, launch
  applications)?
- Do assistants have to be identified
  ahead of time, or can individuals be
  "promoted" during the live event?

CONTENT WINDOWS   NOTES
  CONSIDERATIONS

- Can content be added during the live
  event?
- How are plug-ins managed?
- What file formats can be used?
- Are web and/or PowerPoint™ anima-
  tions viewable?
- Can you write on top of animated
  content?

MISCELLANEOUS FEATURE   NOTES
  CONSIDERATIONS

MISCELLANEOUS FEATURE   NOTES
  CONSIDERATIONS

APPENDIX B

Synchronous Classroom Management Checklists

Minimum Software and Hardware Requirements

☐ 133MHz—preferably 200MHz

☐ 32 MB of RAM—preferably 64

☐ 10 MB hard-drive space

☐ 16-bit sound card (with speaker and microphone)

☐ 800 x 600 resolution monitor (at least fifteen-inch)

☐ 56K modem with Internet connection at 40K bps or higher
(having a 56K modem does not guarantee a 56K connection)

Materials Checklist

☐ Course description

☐ Prework instructions, including any specific URLs

☐ Participant workbook

☐ Synchronous classroom job aid for participants

☐ Leader's guide for trainer and producer

☐ Prepared text files for exercises for producer (if necessary)

☐ Prepared text files for exercises for trainer (if necessary)

☐ Synchronous classroom files with synchronous course slides
and activities (must be uploaded to the server before class)

At Least Two Weeks Before the Class

Have you . . .

☐ Reserved the resources you will need?

☐ Reviewed the course content?

☐ Prepared any necessary reference materials or additional materials?

☐ Created a plan to handle minor technical support issues?

☐ Created a back-up plan in case of major technical problems?

☐ Coordinated timing and tasks with your producer?

☐ Coordinated the schedule with your system administrator?

☐ Emailed a program overview to participants (including technical requirements and instructions)?

☐ Emailed to confirm that participants are still planning to attend the class?

☐ Emailed a program description to participants?

☐ Watched a recorded version of the class (if available)?

☐ Had a dress rehearsal?

One Week Before the Class

Have you . . .

☐ Created and confirmed the final participant list?

☐ Scheduled the event and enrolled this participant group?

☐ Distributed the participant workbooks, prework, and any self-study instructions?

☐ (If necessary) Followed up with participants who have not completed the prework assignments?

On the Day of Class

Have you . . .

☐ Checked your own equipment?

☐ Checked in with participants to verify attendance and answer any last-minute questions?

Forty-Five Minutes Prior to Class

Have you . . .

☐ Hung a "Do Not Disturb" sign on your door?

☐ Cleared your teaching area of distractions?

☐ Arranged your PC window (1024 by 728 screen resolution; whiteboard and chat area both visible)?

☐ Logged on for class at least thirty minutes before the start?

☐ (Optional) Logged on as a participant on another PC?

☐ Conducted an audio check for arriving participants?

☐ Encouraged arriving participants to use the chat area?

After the Class

Have you . . .

☐ Watched and published your recordings?

☐ Followed up with participants who had trouble?

☐ Written a self-assessment of the event?

Recommended Resources for Synchronous and Blended e-Learning

Websites

These links are provided for your information only. They do not necessarily reflect an endorsement of the site. Although links are checked from time to time, the link may have changed since our last check.

- ASTD's Roadmap to E-Learning: *www.astd.org/virtual_community/Comm_elrng_rdmap/roadmap.html*
- Brandon-hall.com: *www.brandon-hall.com*. Provides objective information and research about using technology for learning.
- Distance-Educator.com: *www.distance-educator.com*. Provides information and access to expertise on distance teaching and learning.
- InSync Training: *www.insynctraining.com*. Tips, techniques, and resources for synchronous learning.
- Learning Circuits: *www.learningcircuits.org*. ASTD's online magazine all about eLearning
- Masie Center: *www.masie.com*. The Masie Center is an international think tank located in Saratoga Springs, New York. The Center is dedicated to exploring the intersection of learning and technology.

- The Studio of Saul Carliner: *http://saulcarliner.home.att.net/*. Content development for the workplace.

Books

2000/2001 ASTD Distance Learning Yearbook: The Newest Trends and Technologies by Karen Mantyla (ASTD, 2001).

This handy one-volume resource includes information on creating distance learning proposals and pilot programs; Internet-based training, videoconferencing, and other technologies; setting up and administering a program; career development for trainers; and more.

The AMA Handbook of E-Learning: Effective Design, Implementation, and Technology Solutions by George Piskurich (Ed.) (American Management Association, 2003).

This authoritative sourcebook is a timely decision-making tool for companies making the transition to (or already using) e-learning. Featuring all-original contributions from high-profile practitioners and renowned theorists, the book reveals how top companies are implementing and using this crucial employee development tool.

Web-Based Training: Using Technology to Design Adult Learning Experiences (2nd ed.) by Margaret Driscoll (Pfeiffer, 2002).

This book is written for instructional designers, adult educators, training and human resource managers, and workplace educators developing their first web-based training program.

APPENDIX D

A Glossary of Terms

Awareness of the following web-based learning terms will assist you as you create effective synchronous programs:

Application Viewing/Sharing. A feature that allows the facilitator to share applications with participants. For example, a facilitator may use application sharing to have participants alter a Microsoft Excel document, even though the participants do not have Excel installed on their own computers.

Asynchronous. "Asynchronous" refers to instruction that is not constrained by geography or time. Everyone involved in an asynchronous activity performs his or her part on his or her own time.

Audio. The most common synchronous medium. Using audio, the facilitator and participants can talk to one another over the Internet or through a phone bridge (teleconferencing). One-way audio (only the facilitator can speak) or two-way audio (both the facilitator and participants can speak) is available in most synchronous software packages.

Bandwidth. The speed at which information is transferred via modem or other network-access device to Internet users. The greater the bandwidth, the more quickly the data (audio, video, text) reaches the user.

Blended Learning.   A combination—or blend—of different learning technologies. Blended learning is becoming increasingly common with the availability of both synchronous and asynchronous web-learning options. An example is a course that consists of an asynchronous web module that covers content and a follow-up synchronous module that allows participants to apply the content.

Breakout Sessions.   A feature available in some synchronous software packages that allows the facilitator to break a class into smaller groups. Participants are able to interact within their smaller groups and rejoin the main classroom to share their findings with the whole group.

Chat.   A real-time text conversation between users over the Internet. Whatever a user types is displayed on the other users' screens as it is entered. Some synchronous software packages offer a chat function; it provides an avenue for interaction between participants and trainer. Chat dialogues can often be saved for later reference.

Computer-Assisted Instruction.   A term used commonly in education to describe instruction in which a computer is used as a learning tool.

Computer-Based Learning.   An all-encompassing term used to describe any computer-delivered learning, including CD-ROM and the World Wide Web.

Desktop Learning.   Any learning delivered by computer at the participant's desk.

Desktop Video Conferencing.   A real-time conference using live pictures between two or more people who communicate via computer on a network.

Discussion Board. An asynchronous feature that allows participants to post messages and reply to messages by topic. Discussion boards are different from chat in that they are not real-time.

e-Learning. A term used to describe electronically delivered learning methods such as CD-ROM, web-based learning, online assessments, web-based reinforcement tools, and online coaching.

Evaluation. A test-like feature that enables a trainer to conduct pre- and post-session assessments and to monitor participants' understanding of course material as it is being presented. Assessment results can be automatically tabulated and saved.

Extranet. A website for existing customers rather than the general public. It can provide access to paid research, current inventories, internal databases, and virtually any other information that is published for a limited audience. An extranet uses the public Internet as its transmission system but requires passwords to gain access.

Firewall. A set of software programs that keeps a network secure. Firewalls are widely used to give users access to the Internet in a secure fashion as well as to separate a company's public web server from its internal network. They are also used to keep internal network segments secure—for example, a research or accounting subnet that might be vulnerable to snooping from within.

HTML (Hypertext Markup Language). The authoring language used to create documents that can be viewed via the World Wide Web.

Hyperlinks. An element in an electronic document that can link to another place either within the same document or in a different document. Typically the user clicks the hyperlink to follow the link.

Internet-Based Training.   Training that can be conducted over the Internet. Usually this is done with the World Wide Web, but email correspondence courses and file transfers also fall into this category.

ISP (Internet Service Provider).   An organization that provides access to the Internet. Examples include America Online® and Earthlink®. For a fee, a website can be created and maintained on the ISP's server, allowing a smaller organization to have a presence on the web with its own domain name.

Intranet.   An in-house website that serves the employees of an organization. Although intranet pages may link to the Internet, an intranet is not a site accessed by the general public. Intranets use the same communications protocols and hypertext links as the web and thus provide a standard way of distributing information internally and extending the application worldwide at the same time.

Intranet-Based Training.   Training provided through a company's internal network. Web browsers are used to access company pages. The primary characteristic is that content is accessible only within the company's internal network.

Learning Management System.   Software that automates the administration of training events.

Learning Technologies.   Any tool or technology that facilitates learning. This includes classroom, correspondence, books, audiotapes, teleconferencing, interactive television, CD-ROM, and the World Wide Web.

Online Learning.   An all-encompassing term that refers to any learning done with a computer over a network, including a company's intranet, the company's local area network (LAN), and the Internet.

Pacing/Comprehension.   A feature in synchronous software programs that allows participants to continually appraise the trainer on the pace and clarity of the delivery.

Plug-In.   Software typically downloaded from the web that enables the user to read, hear, or view something. Examples of plug-ins include Adobe Acrobat® Reader to view documents, Real-Player® audio to listen to sound or music, and Flash™ to view animation and graphics and listen to audio.

Portal.   A web "supersite" that provides a variety of services, including web searching, news, white and yellow pages directories, free email, discussion groups, online shopping, and links to other sites. Web portals are the web equivalent of original online services such as CompuServe® and AOL. Although the term was initially used to refer to general-purpose sites, it is increasingly being used to refer to market sites that offer the same services, but only to a particular industry, such as banking, insurance, or computers.

Producer.   A person who assists the trainer during live synchronous events by acting as an "extra set of hands." In addition to training responsibilities, the producer handles technical support so that the trainer can focus on instruction. The producer does not need to be in the same physical location as the trainer.

Record/Playback.   Feature that allows the trainer and participant to record synchronous events, play them back later, and edit them into asynchronous sessions. This feature benefits individuals who miss sessions and allows quick creation of asynchronous learning content.

Self-Paced Learning.   Learning that is taken at a time, pace, and place that are chosen by the participant. Generally, there is no interaction (synchronous or asynchronous) with a trainer.

Survey/Poll.   A quick way to check the pulse of the class. Questions can be true-false, multiple-choice, or other formats.

Synchronous Learning.   This term refers to instruction that is led by a trainer in real time. Examples of synchronous interactions include traditional trainer-led classrooms, conference calls, instant messengers, videoconferences, whiteboard sessions, and synchronous online classrooms/classroom software.

Synchronous Web Browsing.   Element that allows trainers or participants to bring the class to a specific Internet or intranet site. A variation of the feature allows the use of browsers to run short, self-paced exercises on the Internet or intranet as part of a synchronous session.

VoIP.   Technically, this is "Voice delivered over the Internet Protocol." This means sending voice information in digital form using the Internet.

Web Streaming.   Live playback of audio or video files on the web. Usually involves a plug-in or applications program to execute the media file.

Webinars.   A Webinar uses a collaborative tool to deliver a Web-based presentation that features an expert speaker.

Whiteboard.   An application used in synchronous interactive web conferencing that allows documents and content materials to be posted on the screen for all participants to see. The participants see the information being changed on their screens in real time. Whiteboards work well for visual symbols, charts, and graphs.

About the Author

Jennifer Hofmann is a training consultant who specializes in the design and delivery of synchronous learning. After eight years of managing technology-based training and development initiatives, Jennifer now owns and manages InSync Training, LLC. Her team provides workshops and development services to individuals and organizations looking to implement a synchronous classroom. She has experience using all of the major synchronous platforms.

Jennifer has made many contributions to the ASTD online publication, Learning Circuits (www.learningcircuits.org). She is a regular speaker on synchronous learning at national industry events and has taught the Certified Online Instructor Program at Walden University. Contact Jennifer by sending an email message to jennifer@insynctraining.com.

InSync Training, LLC, is the industry leader in the design, development, and delivery of synchronous training and education. Owned by Jennifer Hofmann, author of The *Synchronous Trainer's Survival Guide*, InSync offers a variety of consulting, development, and delivery services to support synchronous training initiatives. Some of the services provided include:

- Expertise in synchronous training platforms;
- Experienced project management and design team;
- Synchronous facilitation services; and
- Synchronous training workshops, including train-the-trainer live event production services.

InSync is on the Web at www.insynctraining.com or contact Jennifer directly at Jennifer@insynctraining.com.

Feedback

Any feedback, tips, or techniques you can provide will be considered for future publications.

☐ Suggestions for Improvement

☐ Examples and Anecdotes

☐ Tips and Techniques

☐ Useful Resources

☐ Sample Checklists or Job Aids

Please email your feedback directly to the author at Jennifer@insynctraining.com.

Index

A

Application viewing/sharing: defining, 127; software features for synchronous, 22t–23t

Assistant trainer synchronous feature, 25t–26t

Asynchronous classrooms: advantages/disadvantages of, 9–10; defining, 127; delivery method of, 8fig, 9–10

Audio: controlling distractions/interference of, 103; defining, 127; software features for synchronous, 15t; tips on using Internet, 55; troubleshooting non-standard, 96

Audiotapes asynchronous instruction, 9

B

Bandwidth: defining, 127–128; troubleshooting problems with, 93

Bandwidth-intensive media, 96

Blended learning: defining, 128; delivery methods used in, 10–11; recommended resources for synchronous and, 125–126

Breakout rooms: production task of launching, 40; software feature for synchronous, 16t–17t; tips on using, 88

Breakout sessions, 128

C

CD-ROM asynchronous instruction, 9

Centra's Symposium software platform, 13, 23t

Chats: arranging PC window during, 86fig; being flexible/creative in use of, 64–65; described, 62, 128; real-world examples of exercises using, 63–64; software feature for synchronous, 15t–16t; tips for facilitating exercises in, 62–63; troubleshooting tip on, 96

Class size, 65

Colorblind participants, 107

Communicating: collaboration tools for, 59–65; gauging participation in, 55–59; language tips for, 53–55; managing classroom for, 73–75; note on class size and, 65; rules of thumb for, 65–68; using visuals, 49–52; using your voice, 52–53

Communication collaborative tools: advantages of using, 59–60; chat area, 15t–16t, 62–65, 86fig, 96; note on class size and, 65; synchronous whiteboard, 17t–19t, 40, 60–62

Comprehension synchronous feature, 19t–20t

Computer-assisted instruction, 128

Computer-based learning, 128

Content windows synchronous feature, 26t–27t

Correspondence schools, 2

D

"Dead air" time, 67
Desktop learning, 128
Desktop video conferencing, 128
Discussion boards: used in asynchronous instruction, 9; defining, 129; software features for synchronous, 22t
Dyslexic participants, 106–107

E

e-Learning, 129
eConferences, 2
EDT's LearnLinc, 13, 19t, 21t, 24t
Elluminate's vClass, 13, 19t, 26t
eMeetings, 1, 109–110
Emergency protocols, 42–43
Evaluation/testing: defining, 129; software feature for synchronous, 19t–20t
Extranet, 129

F

Feedback synchronous feature, 19t–20t
Firewall, 129
Flash animation, 96

G

Ground rules: as critical to success, 66; establishing, 43; examples of typical, 101–102

H

Handraising synchronous feature, 19t–20t
Harvard Management Communication Letter, 49
High-speed Internet connection, 34
HorizonLive software platform, 13, 17t, 27t
HTML (Hypertext Markup Language), 129
Hyperlinks, 129

I

Individual synchronous coaching, 75
Instruction: asynchronous, 8fig, 9–10, 127; comparing new vs. older delivery methods of, 7–8fig, 9–11; computer-assisted, 128; trainer responsibilities during real time, 30–31

Instructors. *See* Trainers
Internet: dealing with heavy traffic on, 95; high-speed connection to, 34; recommended synchronous learning resources on the, 125–126; synchronous Web browsing on the, 132; VoIP, 132
Internet audio, 55
Internet-based training, 130
InterWise Millennium software platform, 13, 16t, 25t
Intranet, 130
Intranet-based training, 130
ISP (Internet Service Provider), 130

L

Language communication tips, 53–55
Leader guides: design strategies for, 79–80fig; effective use of, 78–80fig; used in producer/trainer collaboration, 44–45, 46fig
Learn How to Learn Online program, 74–75, 99–101, 106
Learners. *See* Participants
Learning: blended, 10–11, 125–126, 128; computer-based, 128; desktop, 128; e-learning, 129; effective environment for, 102–103; online, 130; self-paced, 131; teaching participants how to learn, 74–75, 99–101, 106. *See also* Synchronous learning; Training
Learning events, 112
Learning management system, 130
Learning technologies: defining, 130; history of, 2–3; impact of, 1; leading to trainer challenges, 30; terminology of, 6. *See also* Technologies
LearnLinc software platform, 13, 19t, 21t, 24t
Live video synchronous feature, 21t–22t

M

Managing technology: arranging your PC window, 84–85fig, 86fig; creating seamless production, 83–90; keystrokes/shortcuts for, 87t; making most of medium by, 89–90; real-world example of, 88–89; sharpening "production" skills, 86–89; troubleshooting, 91–96

Millennium software platform, 13, 16t, 25t
Multi-tasking skills, 66

N

Non-standard audio inputs, 96

O

Online learning, 130

P

Pacing/comprehension software feature, 19t–20t, 131
Participant contact list, 35, 74
Participant experience: challenges of, 98–99; class ground rules and, 43, 66, 101–102; effective learning environment and, 102–103; learning how to learn online, 74–75, 99–101, 106; participant guides to enhance, 103–107, 104fig
Participant guides: content of, 105–106; as critical success factor, 103–104; managing participant challenges, 106–107; providing printed copies for participants, 105; real-world example of, 106; sample table of contents for, 104fig
Participant "tech check," 74
Participants: creating interactions/activities for, 66, 67; deciding on objectives for, 12–13; defining, 6; dyslexic/color-blind, 106–107; email confirmation of attendance by, 72; getting them technically up and running, 93–95; identified by name during session, 53–54; individual synchronous coaching of, 75; limiting class size of, 65; managing log-ons by, 71, 72; production task of warming up, 41, 72–73; responding to messages/managing chat from, 40; time zone differences of, 71; time-release trainer instructions to, 55; trainer experience as, 32–33
Participants classroom participation: distractions competing for, 56, 102; how to gauge, 55–56; managing classroom to facilitate, 73–75; reading cues of, 57–58; real-world example of distraction, 56–57; real-world example of reading cues on, 58–59

PlaceWare software platform, 13, 18t
Plug-in, 131
Polls synchronous feature, 19t–20t
Portal, 131
PowerPoint slides, 105
Producer production tasks: listed, 40–42, 72–73; sample page mockup and, 46fig; specific instructions regarding, 42
Producers: defining, 131; factors influencing working with, 38; learning experience improved by, 38–39; production tasks of, 40–42, 46fig, 72–73; responsibilities during session, 39; role of, 37; team-teaching tips for trainer and, 42–44; working without, 44
Producer/trainer collaboration: leader guides for, 44–45, 46fig; sharpening your "production" skills with, 86–89; team-teaching tips for, 42–44; timing milestone in, 45, 79fig
"Production Text" document, 76, 88
"Push to Talk" button, 55

Q

QuestionMark, 20t
Quicktime movies, 96

R

Record/playback software features, 24t–25t, 131
Recovery period, 67–68

S

Self-paced learning, 131
Slides: sample thumbnail, 81fig; sending PowerPoint, 105; tips for presenting, 51–52
SME (subject-matter expert), 110–111
Software. See Synchronous software
Starr, K., 95
Students. See Participants
Surveys: production task of launching, 40; software feature for synchronous, 19t–20t
Symposium software platform, 13
Synchronized web browsing software feature, 23t–24t
Synchronous classroom management: checklists for, 121–123; communicating

with participants, 73–75; determining best length for program, 73; effective use of leader guide, 78–80fig; preparing to facilitate the class, 75–78; real-world example of time/scheduling, 72–73; time and scheduling issues, 70–72

Synchronous classroom preparation checklists: after the class, 78; at least two weeks before the class, 75–77; day of class, 77; forty-five minutes prior to class, 77

Synchronous classroom sessions: creating detailed facilitation plan for, 66–67; ground rules for, 43, 66, 101–102; making recording available of, 75; managing the technology during, 83–96; note on class size of, 65; planning for technology gaps/"dead air" during, 67; preparing to facilitate, 75–78

Synchronous classrooms: challenges for trainers, 29–30; deciding on objectives for participants in, 12–13; delivery method of, 8fig, 10; importance of recovery period following, 67–68; possible problems of, 10; situations for using, 11–12

Synchronous events: continuum of, 110fig; eMeetings, 1, 109–110; learning events, 112; subject-matter expert (SME) to enhance, 110–111; Webinars, 111–112

Synchronous learning: defining, 3, 132; glossary of terms on, 127–132; recommended resources for, 125–126; teaching participants how to learn in, 74–75. See also Learning

Synchronous software: defining features/functionality of, 14; features checklist for, 117–120; features/functionality listed, 15t–27t; issues to consider in selecting, 13; learning management system, 130; plug-in, 131; vendors of, 13

Synchronous software features/functionality: application sharing, 22t–23t; assistant trainer, 25t–26t; audio, 15t; breakout rooms, 16t–17t; chat, 15t–16; content windows, 26t–27t; defining, 14; discussion boards, 22t; live video, 21t–22t; record and playback, 24t–25t; survey/polls/feedback/handraising/pac-

ing/comprehension, 19t–20t; synchronized web browsing, 23t–24t; testing/evaluation, 20t–21t; whiteboards, 17t–19t

Synchronous training: defining, 1; similarities between broadcast production and, 4

Synchronous Web browsing, 132

T

Teachers. See Trainers

"Tech Check," 91–92

Technical problems: production task to deal with, 40; troubleshooting, 91–96

Technical support number, 34–35, 75

Technologies: business team uses of, 1–2; impact of learning, 1; importance of learning the synchronous, 65–66; increasing application of synchronous, 42; managing the, 83–96; troubleshooting, 91–96. See also Learning technologies

Technology gaps/dead air time, 67

"Ten Commandments of Presentations" (Harvard Management Communication Letter), 49–50

Testing/evaluation: defining, 129; software feature for synchronous, 19t–20t

Time zone differences, 71

Traditional classrooms delivery method, 7–8fig, 9

Trainer profile: job description of, 31–33; responsibilities during real time instruction, 30–31

Trainer workstation environment: computer drawing tablet, 37; high-speed Internet connection, 34; participant contact list, 35, 74; pitcher of water, 37; powerful computer/additional computer, 35–36; private,soundproof room/do not disturb sign, 33–34, 35; studio microphone and speakers, 36; telephone, live technical support, 34–35, 75

Trainer/producer collaboration: leader guides for, 44–45, 46fig; sharpening "production" skills with, 86–89; team-teaching tips for, 42–44; timing milestone in, 45, 79fig

Trainers: assisted by producer, 37–44; challenges of synchronous classroom for, 29–30; deciding on objectives for participants in, 12–13; defining, 6; experience as participant by, 32–33; facilitation tips for synchronous, 65–68; language tips for, 53–55; preparation checklists for, 75–78; profile of effective synchronous, 30–33; sharpening production skills, 86–89; team-teaching tips for producers and, 42–44; time-release instructions to participants, 55; virtual office hours by, 75; voice communication tips for, 52–53; working without producers, 44; workstation of synchronous, 33–37

Training: Internet-based, 130; Intranet-based, 130. *See also* Learning

Troubleshooting technology: getting participants up and running, 93–95; losing your bandwidth, 93; rules of thumb for, 96; "Tech Check" for, 91–92

V

vClass software platform, 13, 19t, 26t

Videotapes asynchronous instruction, 9

Virtual classroom interface: how to gauge participant participation in, 55–56; managing classroom to facilitate, 73–75; participant distractions competing for, 56, 102; reading cues on

participant participation, 57–58; types and levels of, 1

Virtual classroom trend, 3–4

Virtual office hours, 75

Visuals for communication: benefits of using, 49–51; general tips for using slides, 51–52; sending PowerPoint slides, 105

Voice communication tips, 52–53

VoIP (voice delivered over Internet protocol), 132

W

Warming-up participants, 41, 72–73

Web portals, 131

Web streaming, 132

Web-based tutorial asynchronous instruction, 9

WebEx software platform, 13

Webinars, 111–112, 132

Whiteboards: described, 60, 132; production task of scribing on, 40; real-world examples of using, 61–62; software feature for synchronous, 17t–19t; tips for facilitating exercises using, 60–61

Z

Zoomerang, 20t

Pfeiffer Publications Guide

This guide is designed to familiarize you with the various types of Pfeiffer publications. The formats section describes the various types of products that we publish; the methodologies section describes the many different ways that content might be provided within a product. We also provide a list of the topic areas in which we publish.

FORMATS

In addition to its extensive book-publishing program, Pfeiffer offers content in an array of formats, from fieldbooks for the practitioner to complete, ready-to-use training packages that support group learning.

FIELDBOOK Designed to provide information and guidance to practitioners in the midst of action. Most fieldbooks are companions to another, sometimes earlier, work, from which its ideas are derived; the fieldbook makes practical what was theoretical in the original text. Fieldbooks can certainly be read from cover to cover. More likely, though, you'll find yourself bouncing around following a particular theme, or dipping in as the mood, and the situation, dictate.

HANDBOOK A contributed volume of work on a single topic, comprising an eclectic mix of ideas, case studies, and best practices sourced by practitioners and experts in the field.

An editor or team of editors usually is appointed to seek out contributors and to evaluate content for relevance to the topic. Think of a handbook not as a ready-to-eat meal, but as a cookbook of ingredients that enables you to create the most fitting experience for the occasion.

RESOURCE Materials designed to support group learning. They come in many forms: a complete, ready-to-use exercise (such as a game); a comprehensive resource on one topic (such as conflict management) containing a variety of methods and approaches; or a collection of like-minded activities (such as icebreakers) on multiple subjects and situations.

TRAINING PACKAGE An entire, ready-to-use learning program that focuses on a particular topic or skill. All packages comprise a guide for the facilitator/trainer and a workbook for the participants. Some packages are supported with additional media—such as video—or learning aids, instruments, or other devices to help participants understand concepts or practice and develop skills.

- *Facilitator/trainer's guide* Contains an introduction to the program, advice on how to organize and facilitate the learning event, and step-by-step instructor notes. The guide also contains copies of presentation materials—handouts, presentations, and overhead designs, for example—used in the program.

- *Participant's workbook* Contains exercises and reading materials that support the learning goal and serves as a valuable reference and support guide for participants in the weeks and months that follow the learning event. Typically, each participant will require his or her own workbook.

ELECTRONIC CD-ROMs and web-based products transform static Pfeiffer content into dynamic, interactive experiences. Designed to take advantage of the searchability, automation, and ease-of-use that technology provides, our e-products bring convenience and immediate accessibility to your workspace.

METHODOLOGIES

CASE STUDY A presentation, in narrative form, of an actual event that has occurred inside an organization. Case studies are not prescriptive, nor are they used to prove a point; they are designed to develop critical analysis and decision-making skills. A case study has a specific time frame, specifies a sequence of events, is narrative in structure, and contains a plot structure—an issue (what should be/have been done?). Use case studies when the goal is to enable participants to apply previously learned theories to the circumstances in the case, decide what is pertinent, identify the real issues, decide what should have been done, and develop a plan of action.

ENERGIZER A short activity that develops readiness for the next session or learning event. Energizers are most commonly used after a break or lunch to stimulate or refocus the group. Many involve some form of physical activity, so they are a useful way to counter post-lunch lethargy. Other uses include transitioning from one topic to another, where "mental" distancing is important.

EXPERIENTIAL LEARNING ACTIVITY (ELA) A facilitator-led intervention that moves participants through the learning cycle from experience to application (also known as a Structured Experience). ELAs are carefully thought-out designs in which there is a definite learning purpose and intended outcome. Each step—everything that participants do during the activity—facilitates the accomplishment of the stated goal. Each ELA includes complete instructions for facilitating the intervention and a clear statement of goals, suggested group size and timing, materials required, an explanation of the process, and, where appropriate, possible variations to the activity. (For more detail on Experiential Learning Activities, see the Introduction to the *Reference Guide to Handbooks and Annuals*, 1999 edition, Pfeiffer, San Francisco.)

GAME A group activity that has the purpose of fostering team spirit and togetherness in addition to the achievement of a pre-stated goal. Usually contrived—undertaking a desert expedition, for example—this type of learning method offers an engaging means for participants to demonstrate and practice business and interpersonal skills. Games are effective for team building and personal development mainly because the goal is subordinate to the process—the means through which participants reach decisions, collaborate, communicate, and generate trust and understanding. Games often engage teams in "friendly" competition.

ICEBREAKER A (usually) short activity designed to help participants overcome initial anxiety in a training session and/or to acquaint the participants with one another. An icebreaker can be a fun activity or can be tied to specific topics or training goals. While a useful tool in itself, the icebreaker comes into its own in situations where tension or resistance exists within a group.

INSTRUMENT A device used to assess, appraise, evaluate, describe, classify, and summarize various aspects of human behavior. The term used to describe an instrument depends primarily on its format and purpose. These terms include survey, questionnaire, inventory, diagnostic, survey, and poll. Some uses of instruments include providing instrumental feedback to group members, studying here-and-now processes or functioning within a group, manipulating group composition, and evaluating outcomes of training and other interventions.

Instruments are popular in the training and HR field because, in general, more growth can occur if an individual is provided with a method for focusing specifically on his or her own behavior. Instruments also are used to obtain information that will serve as a basis for change and to assist in workforce planning efforts.

Paper-and-pencil tests still dominate the instrument landscape with a typical package comprising a facilitator's guide, which offers advice on administering the instrument and interpreting the collected data, and an initial set of instruments. Additional instruments are available separately. Pfeiffer, though, is investing heavily in e-instruments. Electronic instrumentation provides effortless distribution and, for larger groups particularly, offers advantages over paper-and-pencil tests in the time it takes to analyze data and provide feedback.

LECTURETTE A short talk that provides an explanation of a principle, model, or process that is pertinent to the participants' current learning needs. A lecturette is intended to establish a common language bond between the trainer and the participants by providing a mutual frame of reference. Use a lecturette as an introduction to a group activity or event, as an interjection during an event, or as a handout.

MODEL A graphic depiction of a system or process and the relationship among its elements. Models provide a frame of reference and something more tangible, and more easily remembered, than a verbal explanation. They also give participants something to "go on," enabling them to track their own progress as they experience the dynamics, processes, and relationships being depicted in the model.

ROLE PLAY A technique in which people assume a role in a situation/scenario: a customer service rep in an angry-customer exchange, for example. The way in which the role is approached is then discussed and feedback is offered. The role play is often repeated using a different approach and/or incorporating changes made based on feedback received. In other words, role playing is a spontaneous interaction involving realistic behavior under artificial (and safe) conditions.

SIMULATION A methodology for understanding the interrelationships among components of a system or process. Simulations differ from games in that they test or use a model that depicts or mirrors some aspect of reality in form, if not necessarily in content. Learning occurs by studying the effects of change on one or more factors of the model. Simulations are commonly used to test hypotheses about what happens in a system—often referred to as "what if?" analysis—or to examine best-case/worst-case scenarios.

THEORY A presentation of an idea from a conjectural perspective. Theories are useful because they encourage us to examine behavior and phenomena through a different lens.

TOPICS

The twin goals of providing effective and practical solutions for workforce training and organization development and meeting the educational needs of training and human resource professionals shape Pfeiffer's publishing program. Core topics include the following:

Leadership and Management

Communication and Presentation

Coaching and Mentoring

Training and Development

e-Learning

Teams and Collaboration

OD and Strategic Planning

Human Resources

Consulting